COMPREHENSIVE RESEARCH
AND STUDY GUIDE

Poets of
World War I

Wilfred Owen
&
Isaac Rosenberg

BLOOM'S
MAJOR
POETS

EDITED AND WITH AN INTRODUCTION
BY HAROLD BLOOM

Poets of World War I

Wilfred Owen

&

Isaac Rosenberg

BLOOM'S *MAJOR* POETS

EDITED AND WITH AN INTRODUCTION
BY HAROLD BLOOM

© 2002 by Chelsea House Publishers, a subsidiary of
Haights Cross Communications.

Introduction © 2002 by Harold Bloom.

Printed and bound in the United States of America.

First Printing
1 3 5 7 9 8 6 4 2

Library of Congress Cataloging-in-Publication Data
Poets of WWI / Harold Bloom, editor.
        p. cm. —(Bloom's major poets)
    Includes bibliographical references and index.
    ISBN 0-7910-5932-4 (alk. paper)
    1.English poetry—20th century—History and criticism—
Handbooks, manuals, etc. 2. World War, 1914–1918—Literature
and the war—Handbooks, manuals, etc. 3. Soldiers' writings,
English—History and criticism—Handbooks, manuals, etc.
4. War poetry, English—History and criticism—Handbooks,
manuals, etc. I. Title: Poets of World War I. II. Title: Poets of World
War One. III. Bloom, Harold. IV. Series.

PR605.W65 P63 2001
821".91209358—dc21   2001028515

Chelsea House Publishers
1974 Sproul Road, Suite 400
Broomall, PA 19008-0914

The Chelsea House World Wide Web address is
http://www.chelseahouse.com

Series Editor: Matt Uhler

Contributing Editor: Kate Cambor

Produced by Publisher's Services, Santa Barbara, California

Contents

User's Guide

This volume is designed to present biographical, critical, and biblio-graphical information on the author's best-known or most important poems. Following Harold Bloom's editor's note and introduction is a detailed biography of the author, discussing major life events and important literary accomplishments. A thematic and structural analysis of each poem follows, tracing significant themes, patterns, and motifs in the work.

A selection of critical extracts, derived from previously published mate-rial from leading critics, analyzes aspects of each poem. The extracts consist of statements from the author, if available, early reviews of the work, and later evaluations up to the present. A bibliography of the author's writings (including a complete list of all books written, cowritten, edited, and translated), a list of additional books and articles on the author and the work, and an index of themes and ideas in the author's writings conclude the volume.

~

Harold Bloom is Sterling Professor of the Humanities at Yale University and Henry W. and Albert A. Berg Professor of English at the New York University Graduate School. He is the author of over 20 books, including *Shelley's Mythmaking* (1959), *The Visionary Company* (1961), *Blake's Apocalypse* (1963), *Yeats* (1970), *A Map of Misreading* (1975), *Kabbalah and Criticism* (1975), *Agon: Toward a Theory of Revisionism* (1982), *The American Religion* (1992), *The Western Canon* (1994), and *Omens of Millennium: The Gnosis of Angels, Dreams, and Resurrection* (1996). *The Anxiety of Influence* (1973) sets forth Professor Bloom's provocative theory of the literary relationships between the great writers and their predecessors. His most recent books include *Shakespeare: The Invention of the Human*, a 1998 National Book Award finalist, and *How to Read and Why*, which was published in 2000.

Professor Bloom earned his Ph.D. from Yale University in 1955 and has served on the Yale faculty since then. He is a 1985 MacArthur Founda-tion Award recipient, served as the Charles Eliot Norton Professor of Poetry at Harvard University in 1987–88, and has received honorary degrees from the universities of Rome and Bologna. In 1999, Professor Bloom received the prestigious American Academy of Arts and Letters Gold Medal for Criticism.

Currently, Harold Bloom is the editor of numerous Chelsea House volumes of literary criticism, including the series BLOOM'S NOTES, BLOOM'S MAJOR DRAMATISTS, BLOOM'S MAJOR NOVELISTS, MAJOR LITERARY CHARACTERS, MODERN CRITICAL VIEWS, MODERN CRITICAL INTERPRETATIONS, and WOMEN WRITERS OF ENGLISH AND THEIR WORKS.

Editor's Note

My Introduction emphasizes the ironical strength of the poetry of Wilfred Owen and Isaac Rosenberg.

As there are almost 30 critical excerpts upon some eight poems by the two poets covered in this volume, I will commend only some particular ones in this note.

The poets Dylan Thomas and Ted Hughes both illuminate Wilfred Owen's masterpiece, "Strange Meeting." Dominic Hibberd adeptly explores Owen's attempts to reconcile his romantic inheritance with his Sassoon-influenced view of war in "Anthem for a Doomed Youth" while David Daiches usefully comments upon Owen's diction.

While several critics concur that Rosenberg lacked the literary inheritance that his contemporaries shared, Horace Gregory, David Daiches, and Jean Liddiard, all provide insights into Rosenberg's isolation from these contemporaries. Finally, I find Joseph Cohen, Marius Bewley, and Paul Fussell all rigorously helpful in appreciating the uniqueness of Isaac Rosenberg, at his most compelling.

Introduction

HAROLD BLOOM

Of the two poets surveyed in this little volume, Wilfred Owen clearly remains the most eminent. Killed in action at twenty-five, the age when tuberculosis ended his precursor, John Keats, Owen nevertheless established himself as a major poet. Besides the four poems commented upon in this anthology, Owen's best work would include "Insensibility," "Greater Love," "Arms and the Boy," and the early, very Keatsian "From My Diary, July 1914." Other critics might choose additional poems, with reason, since Owen's poignance and eloquence are unceasing. Though William Butler Yeats was a considerable influence upon Owen, the great Anglo-Irish poet manifested a singular blindness towards Owen's work. Omitting Owen from *The Oxford Book of Modern Verse,* Yeats defended his decision by calling Owen "unworthy of the poet's corner of a country newspaper" because "he is all blood, dirt, and sucked sugar stick." That is mere abuse, but Yeats more formal explanation is still a shocker:

> . . . passive suffering is not a theme for poetry. In all the great tragedies, tragedy is a joy to the man who dies… If war is necessary in our time and place, it is best to forget its suffering as we do the discomfort of fever . . .

In the Foreword to his anthology, *War Poems* (1999), John Hollander observes rather that war poetry represents a "tremendously varied response to an age-old human theme." For Wilfred Owen, the poetry was in the pity, distinctly not a Yeatsian attitude. I wonder though if a complex irony, rather than pity, is not Owen's true mode:

> I went hunting wild
> After the wildest beauty in the world,
> Which lies not calm in eyes, or braided hair,
> But mocks the steady running of the hour,
> And if it grieves, grieves richlier than here.

***

> For his teeth seem for laughing round an apple.
> There lurk no claws behind his fingers supple;
> And God will grow no talons at his heels,
> Nor antlers through the thickness of his curls.

Friend, be very sure
I shall be better off with plants that share
More peaceably the meadow and the shower.
Soft rains will touch me,— as they could touch
once,
And nothing but the sun shall make me ware.

Perhaps a fatal irony is the essence of war poetry. Simonides (556–468 BCE) achieves ironic perfection in his elegy for the Spartan heroes:

Go tell the Spartans, thou that passest by
That here obedient to their laws we lie.
(Translated by W. L. Bowles)

Isaac Rosenberg, poet-painter killed at twenty-eight, at his rare best transcends even Wilfred Owen's ironies, and suggests the prophetic mode of William Blake:

A worm fed on the heart of Corinth,
Babylon and Rome:
Not Paris raped tall Helen,
But this incestuous worm,
Who lured her vivid beauty
To his amorphous sleep.
England! famous as Helen
Is thy betrothal sung
To him the shadowless,
More amorous than Solomon.

The worm, at once death and the devil, is also war itself, and the prophecy applies readily to an America entering upon the Third Millennium, still addicted to guns, and to an unofficial yet prevalent religion of violence. ❦

Biography of
Wilfred Owen

Perhaps the best known of the war poets, Wilfred Owen was only 25 when he died. He was born in Oswestry on March 18, 1893, into a comfortable, middle-class family, the eldest of the four children of Tom Owen, a railway official, and his wife Susan, to whom Wilfred was devoted all his life.

In 1906 the family moved to Shrewsbury, where Wilfred was educated at the Technical School. He excelled at botany and English literature in particular. His interest in poetry—especially that of Keats—continued to grow, as did his fascination with religion. After failing to win a scholarship to London University in 1911, Owen accepted an appointment as assistant to the vicar of Dunsden, near Reading. Eighteen months later, he again failed to win a scholarship to University College, Reading.

As a result of this setback, coupled with mounting tension between him and the vicar, and a subsequent illness, Owen decided to go to France and teach English part-time at the Berlitz School. Over the next two years, Wilfred came to love France and its culture and finally seemed to find the happiness for which he had been looking. Unfortunately, he had barely discovered this new contentment, when on August 4, 1914, Germany invaded Belgium and war was declared.

Owen's response to the outbreak of war was initially ambivalent. He was clearly influenced by his conversations with Laurent Tailhade, a 59-year-old French pacifist, aesthete, duelist, and poet, whom he had met while in France; Owen wrote to his mother at the end of August 1914: "I can do no service to anybody by agitating for news or making dole over the slaughter. On the contrary I adopt the perfect English custom of dealing with an offender: a Frenchman duels with him; an Englishman ignores him."

Owen remained conflicted about the war but eventually enlisted in the Artists' Rifles on October 21, 1915. After seven months of training in Essex, Owen was commissioned into the Manchester Regiment and underwent further training. After spending Christmas at home, on December 29 he crossed to France. In the second week of January 1917 he led his platoon into the battle of the Somme; he told his mother in a letter, "Those fifty hours were the agony of my happy life."

In the middle of March, Owen fell through a shell-hole into a cellar and was trapped there for three days. This experience is assumed to have contributed to the dark images of an underworld in many of his later poems. After Owen was rescued, he was sick enough that he was allowed a brief rest before he rejoined his battalion and once again found himself in the thick of intense fighting.

Although he escaped serious injuries, the experience was taking its toll. On May 1, his commanding officer thought he was behaving strangely. Owen was eventually diagnosed as suffering from neurasthenia (shellshock) and sent to the Craiglockhart War Hospital on the outskirts of Edinburgh, Scotland.

This turned out to be one of the most fortunate events of Owen's brief life. His doctor believed Owen had lost contact with real life; the doctor sought to re-establish this connection by means of a "work-cure." Owen's work involved contributing to—and eventually editing—the hospital magazine, *The Hydra*.

The Hydra printed two of Owen's poems and four by his fellow patient Siegfried Sassoon. By the time Sassoon arrived at Craiglockhart in July 1917, he already had a reputation as a poet, an infantry officer of exceptional courage, and the author of an "open letter" to his commanding officer protesting the prolongation of the war "by those who have the power to end it." Wilfred Owen was profoundly impressed by Sassoon's "trench sketches" in his just-published book, *The Old Huntsman and Other Poems;* Owen told his mother, "Shakespeare reads vapid after these."

Owen introduced himself to Sassoon, thus beginning an important and productive literary friendship. The older poet, Sassoon, helped Wilfred channel his memories of battle into poems and raised the young man's confidence. Owen's health returned, and in October a medical board determined that he was fit for light duties.

In November 1917, he left for three weeks' leave in London where, with introductions from Sassoon, he met the writer Robert Graves and the art dealer and critic Robert Ross. Ross in turn introduced him to some of his literary friends: the novelists Arnold Bennett and

H. G. Wells among them. A number of Ross's friends were homosexual, as was Sassoon. Owen apparently shared their sexual orientation, although there is still some question as to whether or not he ever entered into a physical relationship with another man.

Owen was assigned to light duties at an officers' hotel in Scarborough; he returned to France in September 1918. These twelve months after leaving Craiglockhart were the most creative period of Owen's career. Buoyed by the encouragement of his new literary friends and occupied by only light duties, Owen was able to develop and express his own distinctive vision of the war. In 1918 five of his poems were published—the only five he was to see in print.

That autumn he returned to the front. In October, he won the Military Cross. One week before the Armistice, on the morning of November 4, 1918, while attempting to move his company of the 2nd Manchesters across the Oise and Sambre Canal near Ors, Wilfred Owen was shot and killed. ❀

Thematic Analysis of
"Dulce et Decorum Est"

Drafted in October 1917 while the poet was recovering from shell-shock at Craiglockhart Hospital, "Dulce et Decorum Est," is one of Wilfred Owen's most popular World War I poems.

During this stay at Craiglockhart, Owen first made the acquaintance of fellow poet and soldier Siegfried Sassoon. Sassoon's poetry about the war possessed an unflinching, direct language and style that profoundly influenced the young Owen, whose work up to this point had displayed the romantic flourishes and lush imagery one would expect from someone who idealized Keats and Shelley. Sassoon recalls criticizing "the over-luscious writing in his immature pieces" and challenging "the almost embarrassing sweetness in the sentiment" in some of the work Owen showed him.

A look at earlier versions of "Dulce et Decorum Est"—there were four drafts in all—show Owen attempting to develop his critique of the war by adopting a language and tone more appropriate to the nightmarish scenes he had witnessed as a soldier in the trenches. Whether this was a direct result of Sassoon's criticism or caused by his own developing poetic sensibility, Owen increasingly chose to contrast the ugliness of the fighting experience with the beauty it was destroying. For instance, in the final version of "Dulce et Decorum Est," Owen removed the following lines, which had appeared in every earlier version:

> And think how, once, his face was like a bud,
> Fresh as a country rose, and pure [also clean/clar/keen], and young,—

He then replaced them with lines intended to emphasize dramatically the violence and profanity of war:

> Obscene as cancer, bitter as the cud
> Of vile, incurable sores on innocent tongues,—

This shift in successive drafts of "Dulce et Decorum Est" from reliance on more conventional poetic attitudes to more urgent, realistic idioms evoked the hideous death by gas that claimed the lives of so many young soldiers—and it revealed Owen's transformation into a modern poet with a distinctive voice.

In a letter to his mother, Susan Owen, Wilfred Owen described "Dulce et Decorum Est" simply as "a gas poem," but this statement does little to convey the full range of poetic and thematic issues the poem addresses. The lines do indeed capture the few, desperate moments before and during a gas attack, as soldiers scramble to put on the masks and protective gear that stand between them and an agonizing death. The title comes from a Latin phrase in Horace, meaning "It is sweet and meet to die for one's country. Sweet! And Decorous!"; this title suggests that Owen sought to do more than chronicle the event. His goal was to attack the concept that sacrifice is sacred; he hoped to destroy the glamorized decency of the war.

Jingoistic sentiments were widely circulated in the popular pro-war propaganda and poetry that filled the pages of newspapers and magazines throughout England. Owen even had a particular pro-war poet in mind when he first composed "Dulce et Decorum Est": in earlier versions, the poem is addressed "To a Certain Poetess," which is now understood as referring to a Miss Jessie Pope, a popular and prolific journalist and author of a number of recruiting poems during the Great War. "My friend" in line 25 of the final version is presumed to refer to her.

Much of the movement and development in "Dulce et Decorum Est" stems from the tension that Owen establishes between the united suffering as a group, on the one hand, and on the other hand, the isolated, subjective experience of the individual when he is most alone—namely, at his own violent death.

The first stanza presents a scene saturated with misery, as Owen uses images of physical deprivation and deterioration usually associated with old age and poverty to convey the unalleviated and inescapable conditions of the life of a soldier. The soldiers are "Bent double, like old beggars under sacks," "coughing like hags." They go lame, blind, deaf, and yet continue to march, not in the hopes of achieving some noble aim, but rather simply toward some brief respite from physical exhaustion. Their sensory depletion is such that not even "the hoots / Of tired, outstripped Five-Nines that dropped behind" instills fear.

However the company is jolted out of their ambulatory state when the gas attack begins: "Gas! Gas! Quick, boys!—An ecstasy of fumbling." The group is saved just in time by their nimble responses—

but then the narrator notices that one among them has not managed to put his gas mask on in time. Instantly, this soldier is set apart from the other men; the narrator observes his panicked reaction from behind the life-saving panels of his own mask. This distance means the difference between life and death.

Owen's method of dramatic description seeks to make the physical and psychological suffering of the war more vivid to the reader, who is invited to share the eyewitness perspective of the narrator. After the opening paragraph, "Dulce et Decorum Est" focuses exclusively on the individual agony, in the manner of the cinema close-up, while simultaneously insisting that the spectator cannot adequately imagine the experience. Despite the almost hyperbolical accumulation of detail, there is something inconceivable about a death so horrible, and so for the narrator as well as the reader, the experience is reduced to a dream. "If in some smothering dreams . . . ," Owen writes, and then later on line 21, "If you could hear . . ."; he is trying to convey the horror of this death to those who were not there to witness it, but he knows deep down the futility of his efforts.

The ghastly final moments of the soldier's life unfolds in the surreal landscape of the gas attack, which turns the visual field into a misty netherworld of "thick green light, / As under a green sea." The image of the dying man's body being carted off as the narrator walks behind it is relived again and again in the narrator's dreams. The contrast between this dream-like setting and the violent and graphic images and sounds of death—"guttering," "choking," "drowning," "writhing," "hanging," "gargling"—allow Owen to further underscore the gap between the reality and fantasy of war, a gap that is epitomized for him by the facile use of the old lie "Dulce et decorum est / Pro patria mori." ❀

Critical Views on
"Dulce et Decorum Est"

[This selection from one of Owen's letters was reprinted in a memoir by his friend Edmund Blunden (1896–1974), a writer and poet. Among Blunden's most famous works are those dealing with English rural life or the experience of trench warfare (*Poems 1913 and 1914* and the memoir *Undertones of War*). Later in his life, Blunden became known as a leading authority on the English Romantic poets. This extract suggests the lingering importance of Owen's vision of war and the destruction it brings.]

"⟨. . .⟩ The other day I read a biography of Tennyson, which says he was unhappy, even in the midst of his fame, wealth, and domestic serenity. Divine discontent! I can quite believe he never knew happiness for one moment such as I have—for one or two moments. But as for misery, was he ever frozen alive, with dead men for comforters? Did he hear the moaning at the Bar, not at twilight and the evening bell only, but at dawn, noon, and night, eating and sleeping, walking and working, always the close moaning of the Bar; the thunder, the hissing, and the whining of the Bar?—Tennyson, it seems, was always a great child. So should I have been, but for Beaumont Hamel. (Not before January 1917 did I write the only lines of mine that carry the stamp of maturity—these:

> But the old happiness is unreturning,
> Boys have no grief as grievous as youth's yearning;
> Boys have no sadness sadder than our hope.) ⟨. . .⟩

—Edmund Blunden, *The Poems of Wilfred Owen* (New York: The Viking Press, 1931): p. 26.

DESMOND GRAHAM ON NARRATIVE DISTANCE

[Desmond Graham is professor at the Department of English Literature, University of Newcastle-upon-Tyne. His works include *Introduction to Poetry* (1968), *Keith Douglas, 1920–1944: A Biography* (1974), and *The Truth of War: Owen, Blunden, Rosenberg* (1984). In this selection Graham discusses the alternate states of seeing and experiencing that drive home the hallucinatory, nightmarish mood of "Dulce et Decorum Est."]

There is no distance between Owen and the narrators of 'Dulce et Decorum Est' and 'Exposure', and no distance between the setting of each poem and the battlefield. Yet there is an extreme distance in the conscious, highly-wrought texture of the poetry. The power of metaphor and timing, and aural patterning, have intervened to mediate directly between the trench scene and the reach of our imaginations. In 'Dulce et Decorum Est', what should be a vision, like that of 'Mental Cases' or 'The Show', turns into the literal and immediate, through direct description and specific references to the trench landscape. This is documentary or reportage, but with Owen's tones and cadences weaving together a harsh commentating knowledge, a narrator's assumed sense of purpose and a dramatic sense that falls away into more lyric cadence, picks up impetus and fades. All this is the expression of the mood: the men's last, driven efforts against exhaustion, their desire to give up in the face of this last demand for activity and their herd-like knowledge that this effort is drawing them away from danger:

> Bent double, like old beggars under sacks,
> Knock-kneed, coughing like hags, we cursed through sludge,
> Till on the haunting flares we turned our backs
> And towards our distant rest began to trudge.
> Men marched asleep. Many had lost their boots
> But limped on, blood-shod. All went lame; all blind;
> Drunk with fatigue; deaf even to the hoots
> Of tired, outstripped Five-Nines that dropped behind.

The double meanings and calculated imprecision of reference are merged into the portrayal of a state where distinctions between inner and outer worlds are blurred. The 'haunting' flares, lighting the scene with their macabre glow, follow and call back the men they will haunt in memory. They 'turn their backs', marching away from the Line, and repudiating its flares and what they mean, defeating the flares' claim to power with a gesture which, the poem will prove, is no more substantial a protection than simply looking away. Distinctions between what is literal and what metaphorical can be sharp: literally, the men had lost their boots; metaphorically, they were like beggars or hags. But also, such distinctions fade: these men are not blind like the sentry blown down the steps of the dug-out in 'The Sentry', yet, physically, their eyes no longer see what is around them, they react only with the reflexes taught them by military command and experience of the trenches; the 'hoots' of the shells are the sound made by five-nines, and they are cries of derision; the arc and descent of the shells is depicted as they fall, 'tired' and 'outstripped', yet they too, in personification, echo the men, not only dropping behind them, but falling back for lack of energy to keep up with the other shells. ⟨. . .⟩

⟨. . .⟩ Nothing will in fact happen to the men of 'Exposure' in the course of the poem; to those of 'Dulce et Decorum Est' a sudden re-awakening of war's violence will bring the demand for energy and for a response to its menace. Suddenly the community of men, all lame, all blind, will be broken as, safe behind his gas mask, the soldier will look on at another who is left without defence, within the power of war's malevolence:

> Gas! GAS! Quick, boys!—An ecstasy of fumbling,
> Fitting the clumsy helmets just in time;
> But someone still was yelling out and stumbling,
> And flound'ring like a man in fire or lime . . .
> Dim, through the misty panes and thick green light,
> As under a green sea, I saw him drowning.

What should be vision or dream is the effect of the gas mask's distortion, the effect of the gas on the light, an exact description of what happened to the gassed man, as the survivor looks on. The distance between the survivor and the gassed soldier will be narrowed as the scene becomes the survivor's nightmare, but what that dream of terror will bring back is not only his own fear but his helplessness, impotently and safely looking on at the man who is beyond anyone's reach: 'In all my dreams, before my helpless sight, / He plunges at me, guttering, choking, drowning.' The plunge towards the dreamer would pull him too under the gas, would bring back his terror, and it would accuse him.

All Owen can do is to direct this impotence outwards, to us, facing us with the experience with which, naturally, he cannot cope. This gives no comfort, but the formula which in other circumstances would be self-defence—'if you too had undergone what I underwent you could not accuse me . . . '—that formula is made an active attack:

> If in some smothering dreams you too could pace
> Behind the wagon that we flung him in, . . .
> My friend, you would not tell with such high zest
> To children ardent for some desperate glory,
> The old Lie: Dulce et decorum est
> Pro patria mori.

Having first used all the shaping power of his poem to bring us the sensations and physical horror of a trench scene, Owen makes from what is a poem of guilt, a poem of protest.

> —Desmond Graham, *The Truth of War: Owen, Blunden, Rosenberg*
> (Manchester, England: Carcanet Press, 1984): pp. 57–58, 59–60.

Mark Van Doren on the Pity of War

[Mark Van Doren an influential poet, teacher, and critic, was awarded the Pulitzer Prize for poetry in 1940 for his *Collected Poems*. Van Doren was a respected Professor of English at Columbia University for 39 years and also served as literary editor and reviewer for the *Nation*. A member of both the National Institute of Arts and Letters and the American Academy of Arts and Letters, Van Doren was the author of more than a dozen volumes of poetry as well as several major critical books, including *Shakespeare* (1939), *The Noble Voice: A Study of Ten Great Poems* (1946), and *Nathaniel Hawthorne* (1949). In this 1921 review of Owen's *Poems*, Van Doren discusses Owen's reputation compared with other "war poets."]

One did not believe that any further volumes of war poetry, even anti-war poetry, could come to this country from England and be impressive. It seemed certain that Siegfried Sassoon and Osbert Sitwell, one with his denunciation of generals and the other with his denudation of civilians, had said the last word about incredible nations in factitious conflict. So that an American edition of Wilfred

Owen had to overcome what looked like permanent public inertia. Nor was such an edition especially recommended by the announcement that its original in London had aroused virtually all the critics of any importance there to acclaim Wilfred Owen the poet of the war. America once had heard that Mr. Sassoon was the poet of the war, had read him, and had found him dull. But Wilfred Owen's poems come from England now, and they convince. They make a small volume, yet one that is more sincere in its last line than the average volume is in its whole bulk. The preface, found in an unfinished condition among the soldier's papers after his death, contains among others these three jottings:

> Above all, this book is not concerned with Poetry.
> The subject of it is War, and the pity of War.
> The Poetry is in the pity.

The pieces which follow are rugged, thickly knit, and hoarse with intentional dissonances. Anger, or pity, gathers in each as it proceeds, and discharges accusation at the end:

> If in some smothering dreams, you too could pace
> Behind the wagon that we flung him in,
> And watch the white eyes writhing in his face,
> His hanging face, like a devil's sick of sin,
> If you could hear, at every jolt, the blood
> Come gargling from the froth-corrupted lungs
> Bitten as the cud
> Of vile, incurable sores on innocent tongues—
> My friend, you would not tell with such high zest
> To children ardent for some desperate glory,
> The old Lie: *Dulce et decorum est*
> *Pro patria mori.*

If the poetry of the pity of war ends with Wilfred Owen (as he prayed it would not), it will end in a thoroughly good and memorable book.

—Mark Van Doren, "War and Peace" (Review of *Poems* by Wilfred Owen and *The Waggoner* by Edmund Blunden), *The Nation* (25 May 1921): p. 747.

Thematic Analysis of
"Strange Meeting"

Drafted at some point between January and March 1918, "Strange Meeting" may not have been considered complete by Wilfred Owen. His friend Edmund Blunden has called it "the most remote and intimate, tranquil and dynamic, of all Owen's imaginative statements of war experience," while Siegfried Sassoon once described it as Owen's "passport to immortality, and his elegy to the unknown warriors of all nations." Critics have largely agreed, viewing "Strange Meeting" as one of Owen's most haunting and complex war poems.

"Strange Meeting" is told from the point of view of the narrator who attempts to escape the death and thumping guns by going down into the trenches. Once there, however, he finds that he has descended into Hell, where he is confronted with a man he himself has killed. Unlike the hatred and violence exploding above ground, this underground encounter between the two soldiers from opposing armies and nations is infused with an elegaic sense of reconciliation and regret. There, in the silence of the trench / underworld, the soldier and the stranger can reflect on the larger meaning of the war and the toll it is taking on the young men of Europe.

The use of "strange" in the title could be referring to the fact that enemies are not expected to meet face to face in a spirit of reconciliation but rather in search of revenge. Or Owen could have been using "strange" simply to describe the unusual encounter between the living and the dead.

As in "Dulce et Decorum Est," in "Strange Meeting" Owen deftly fuses the realistic world of the trenches with that of a dream landscape. The subterranean meeting provides a chance to escape from the fighting above as well as a chance to gain a more critical and objective perspective on the fighting.

After a brief prologue describing the narrator's removal from the fighting, the other three stanzas of the poem detail the "strange meeting" between the two men. Initially, the distance between the two figures is maintained by Owen's description of the dead soldier's unpleasant physical condition. His face is ingrained with "a thousand pains," and he looks up at the narrator with "piteous recognition in fixed eyes" while "lifting distressful hands." But in the course of this strange meeting, even the most basic and essential distinctions of war—between "I" and "you," "enemy" and "friend"—will be dislocated and, at least momentarily, overcome. From the moment the two figures in "Strange Meeting" speak, the differences between them fade into the background. "Whatever hope is yours, / Was my life also," the soldier states.

But the focus quickly shifts from an examination of the specific trajectory of these two men's lives to a discussion of the artistic, personal, and historical implications of the war more generally. The pursuit of beauty is no longer possible, the soldier begins, in a world destroyed by war, when future generations have only this bloody legacy and "will go content with what we spoiled / Or, discontent, boil bloody." If he had been left to his pre-war pursuits, the fallen soldier suggests, he would not have been responsible for the deaths of others. And just as he recognizes his responsibility for cutting short the lives and potentials of other men, he talks about his own death as the severing of an unfinished existence: "For by my glee might many men have laughed. / And of my weeping something had been left, / Which must die now."

Youthful idealistic views of war and the myth of the soldier's sacrificial regeneration of his country are replaced by the cynical recognition that no amount of blood will suffice to end the fighting. Redemption and reconciliation seem only a remote possibility, since the men who fought in the war and, therefore, have some insight into the Truth, have been maimed and killed. The work of the poet will remain incomplete and the truth of the war—"The pity of war, the pity war distilled"—will never be told.

As the image of a second Fall, "Strange Meeting" is terrifying in its representation of the ultimate retrogression of humanity and its disintegration of values. In this time of crisis, when "none will break ranks" and nations send their youth to battle like lambs to the slaughter, the role of the poet is forced to undergo a transformation. His new pursuit must be the "truth untold," his function becoming social and political rather than solely personal or aesthetic. And yet the poet's identification with the dead soldier implies the futility of this very endeavor and warns that the truth will remain "untold."

The identity of the stranger has been explained in a number of different ways. Some critics have regarded him as Owen's double, who shares the poet's artistic vision and spiritual destiny. However,

Owen himself, until a late stage of revision, thought of the stranger as "a German conscript," and thus as an enemy counterpart rather than a double or *Doppelgänger*. Still others have set aside the specific political context of the war and seen the enemy as representing every person's alter ego, the evil and aggressive portions of the soul.

In all of these readings of "Strange Meeting," we are left with the idea that war turns human beings not only against each other but also against themselves. Through his experience in the war, the soldier loses his ability to empathize and identify with all men; hence, the physical death represents the spiritual death of both the person and society.

Critics have noted that similar themes of universal brotherhood in the face of death are found in Shelley's *Revolt of Islam* and Keats' *Endymion*, the former perhaps providing the title for Owen's poem. In *Revolt of Islam*, Shelley's narrator, who has lost consciousness as a result of a dangerous wound, wakens to find himself confronted by the enemy soldier who inflicted it:

> And one whose spear had pierced me, leaned beside,
> With quivering lips and humid eyes—and all
> Seemed like some brothers on a journey wide
> Gone forth, whom now strange meeting did befall
> In a strange land . . .

Both *Revolt of Islam* and *Endymion* are concerned with the reconciliation of enemies and the underlying commonality that links all humanity to each other. "Strange Meeting" is thus an example of how Owen's connection to the Romantic tradition could produce a powerfully lyrical and yet unmistakably modern poem.

In addition to its compelling narrative, "Strange Meeting" also stands apart due to its rhythmic structure. One major influence that Owen exerted on the technique of English verse is his development of the half-rhyme. The principle behind this technique is that instead of changing the initial consonant while retaining the vowel sound, the consonantal framework is retained and the vowel changed (groined/groaned; moan/mourn). For Owen the use of half-rhyme gave his work a less "poetic" feel. Achieving this easier, unpretentious, colloquial speech became particularly important for Owen after meeting Sassoon. As John Middleton Murry observed in his 1921 review of *Owen's Collected Poems,* "These assonant endings are indeed the discovery of a genius." Some critics have argued that Owen's use of half-rhyme actually met a more compelling, emotional need and offered a unique expression of that diffidence and lack of self-confidence that he possessed. In constructing these half-rhymes, Owen frequently made sure that the second rhyme was lower in pitch than the first, giving the couplet a "dying fall" that creates a kind of inexorable, muffled beat registering a haunting uneasiness and frustration. ❀

Critical Views on
"Strange Meeting"

DYLAN THOMAS ON OWEN'S DEVELOPMENT AS A POET

[Dylan Thomas, a Welsh poet and prose writer of great renown, was known for his reckless lifestyle and emotional and difficult poetry. In addition to his poetic works, which include *18 Poems* (1934), *Twenty-Five Poems* (1936), and *Deaths and Entrances* (1946), Thomas wrote numerous short stories that appeared in such works as *The Map of Love* (1939), *Portrait of the Artist as a Young Dog* (1940), and *A Child's Christmas in Wales* (1955), as well as BBC radio scripts, two novels, and five published screenplays. In this chapter on Wilfred Owen in *Quite Early One Morning* (1954), a posthumously published collection of critical essays, Thomas writes about the universal quality of Owen's poetry, declaring him "a poet of all times, all places, and all wars."]

⟨. . .⟩ And this time, when, in the words of an American critic, the audiences of the earth, witnessing what well may be the last act of their own tragedy, insist upon chief actors who are senseless enough to perform a cataclysm, the voice of the poetry of Wilfred Owen speaks to us, down the revolving stages of thirty years, with terrible new significance and strength. We had not forgotten his poetry, but perhaps we had allowed ourselves to think of it as the voice of one particular time, one place, one war. Now, at the beginning of what, in the future, may never be known to historians as the "atomic age"—for obvious reasons: there may be no historians—we can see, rereading Owen, that he is a poet of all times, all places, and all wars. There is only one War: that of men against men.

Owen left to us less than sixty poems, many of them complete works of art, some of them fragments, some of them in several versions of revision, the last poem of them all dying away in the middle of a line: "Let us sleep now. . . ." I shall not try to follow his short life, from the first imitations of his beloved Keats to the last prodigious whisper of "sleep" down the profound and echoing tunnels of "Strange Meeting." Mr. Edmund Blunden, in the introduction to his probably definitive edition of the poems, has done that with skill and love. His collected poems make a little, huge book, working— always he worked on his poems like fury, or a poet—from a lush ornamentation of language, brilliantly, borrowed melody, and ingenuous sentiment, to dark, grave, assonant rhythms, vocabulary purged and sinewed, wrathful pity and prophetic utterance. ⟨. . .⟩

It was impossible for him to avoid the sharing of suffering. He could not record a wound that was not his own. He had so very many deaths to die, and so very short a life within which to endure them all. It's no use trying to imagine what would have happened to Owen had he lived on. Owen, at twenty-six or so, exposed to the hysteria and exploded values of false peace. Owen alive now, at the age of fifty-three, and half the world starving. You cannot generalize about age and poetry. A man's poems, if they are good poems, are always older than himself; and sometimes they are ageless. We know that the shape and the texture of his poems would always be restlessly changing, though the purpose behind them would surely remain unalterable; he would always be experimenting technically, deeper and deeper driving towards the final intensity of language: the words behind words. Poetry is, of its nature, an experiment. All poetical impulses are towards the creation of adventure. And adventure is movement. And the end of each adventure is a new impulse to move again towards creation. Owen, had he lived, would never have ceased experiment; and so powerful was the impetus behind his work, and so intricately strange his always growing mastery of words, he would never have ceased to influence the work of his contemporaries. Had he lived, English poetry would not be the same. The course of poetry is dictated by accidents. Even so, he is one of the four most profound influences upon the poets who came after him; the other three being Gerard Manley Hopkins, the later W. B. Yeats, and T. S. Eliot.

—Dylan Thomas, *Quite Early One Morning* (New York: New Directions, 1954): pp. 118–19, 125–26.

TED HUGHES ON THE LEGACY OF OWEN

[Ted Hughes has enjoyed a reputation as a poet of international stature since the publication of his first poetry collection, *The Hawk in the Rain*. Hughes is perhaps best known for Crow, an animal who began appearing in his work in 1967 and was the main character in several volumes of poetry, including *A Crow Hymn, Crow: From the Life and Songs of the Crow*, and *Crow Wakes*. His 1984 appointment as Poet Laureate of England assured his status as a major British poet of the 20th century. Although Hughes has distinguished himself primarily as a poet, he is also respected for his many other literary endeavors. In particular, critics praise his careful editing of the posthumously published work of his late wife, the poet and novelist Sylvia Plath. In this 1964 review of *The Collected Poems of Wilfred Owen*, edited by C. Day Lewis, Hughes discusses how Owen's poetry became a vehicle for a kind of anti-war propaganda that the poet was determined to use against the *real* enemy of the war, namely the jingoistic and violently patriotic sentiments of those who remained in England.]

Wilfred Owen's 20 or so effective poems, all quite short, belong to a brief, abnormal moment in English history, and seem to refer to nothing specific outside it. That moment—the last two years of trench warfare in France, 1916–18—was so privately English (and perhaps German) and such a deeply shocking and formative experience for us that it is easy to see some of the reasons why Yeats dismissed Owen's verse (largely on principle), and why many discriminating American readers find it hard to account for his reputation, and why with the English his reputation is so high.

The particular pathos and heroism and horror of the fighting in France are not imaginable without a full sense of the deaf-and-blind tyranny of jingoism—the outraged rhetorical patriotism-to-the-death, the bluster and propaganda of England's unshaken imperial insolence—of those who remained in England. These were the politicians, financiers, businessmen, all who found themselves too old, or too importantly placed, or too deeply embedded in business, or too much of the wrong sex, fastened like a lid over the men who were rubbished with such incredible, pointless abandon into the trenches. For these men Owen, who died in France a week before the Armistice, determined to become the Voice of Protest.

He had all the gifts ready for it. In 1911 he had started a year as pupil and lay assistant to the vicar of Dunsden, Oxfordshire, and there seems to have been an idea of his taking holy orders. This readiness to give his life to Christ was to be important, as was his talent for righteous wrath and quick sympathy for the oppressed that went with it. "From what I hear from the tight-pursed lips of wolvish ploughmen in their cottages, I might say there is material here for another revolution," he noted.

Then there was his poetic talent—commonplace enough up to 1916—but showing a precocious tendency to the monumental and elegiac on the one hand, and on the other a natural zest for orgies of sensation, carefully nursed in imitation of his idol Keats, that truly seems to have had a special taste for the horrible, a romantic fever for the Gothic and macabre. Then suddenly the unbelievable war was on him, mobilizing these inclinations in him, and in the name of a high, holy cause and supplying the unique material, in the baldest reality, as nothing else could have done.

He worked within a narrow program—not that his times or situation allowed him much alternative, but he did formulate it deliberately. He wanted to oppose the propagandists in England with a propaganda of a finally more powerful kind. He set himself to present the sufferings of the front line, with the youth and millions of deaths and smashed hopes of his whole generation behind him, as vividly and frighteningly as possible, not because they were piteous—in spite of all his misleading talk about "pity"—but because it was wrong, and the crime of fools who could not see because they would not feel.

The enemy was not Germany. The only German in his poems—in "Strange Meeting"—is one he has been made to kill, who calls him "my friend" and who turns out to be himself. The real enemy is that Public Monster of Warmongering Insensibility at home. For England, the Great War was in fact, a kind of civil war (still unfinished—which helps to explain its profound meaning for modern England, its hold on our feelings, and why Owen's poetry is still so relevant). His poems had to be weapons. Nothing in them could be vivid enough, or sorrowful enough; words could never be terrible enough, for the work he had to do. He had an idea of helping his cause along with merciless photographs of the trenches that would be displayed in London. Few poets can ever have written with such urgent, defined, practical purpose. And it is this attitude of managing a vital persuasion which perhaps explains his extraordinary detachment from the agony, his objectivity. He is not saying, "Ah, God, how horrible for us!" but "Look what you've done, look," as he glues the reader's eyes to it.

—Ted Hughes, "The Crime of Fools Exposed" (review of *The Collected Poems of Wilfred Owen*), *New York Times Book Review* (12 April 1964): p. 4.

ELLIOTT B. GOSE JR. ON UNIVERSALITY IN "STRANGE MEETING"

[Elliot Gose is a professor of English at the University of British Columbia, Vancouver, and a frequent contributor to literary journals on various aspects of 19th-century fiction. His works include *Imagination Indulged: The Irrational in the Nineteenth-Century* (1972), *Transformation: Process in Joyce's* Ulysses (1980), and *Mere Creatures: A Study of Modern Fantasy Tales for Children*. In this selection, Gose argues that the "strange meeting" of Owen's poem refers to the narrator's encounter with his primal self from which he has been alienated due to the war. For Gose, then, "Strange Meeting" reflects Owen's larger aim of reacquainting his readers with pity, that emotion that could halt the dehumanizing process of modern warfare.]

The Other's linking of himself with the narrator is an odd one: "Whatever hope *is* yours *was* my life also." Presumably the narrator still has hope because he is new to Hell. But is his *hope* the Other's *life also*? Perhaps because hope is life, as the old saying tells us.

Of his weeping, the Other says, "something had been left which must die now" (that the narrator is dead?). That something, "the truth untold, the pity . . . war distilled" was also the subject of

Owen's well-known preface to his work and provides the key to the narrator's crime, which is revealed in the last lines of the poem.

> "I am the enemy you killed, my friend.
> I knew you in this dark; for so you frowned
> Yesterday through me as you jabbed and
>   killed.
> I parried, but my hands were loath and cold.
> Let us sleep now. . . ."

The narrator has been guilty of a failure of imagination. The Other is not asking him to refrain from fighting; the reason his "hands were loath and cold" when he parried is because the narrator "frowned . . . *through*" him as he "jabbed and killed." The narrator has lost human feeling; instead of fighting the Other as another individual, he has fought him as, let us say, the Enemy, the Boche whom Owen's despised civilian armchair generals hated with such a liberal and impersonal hate. As George Orwell put it in "Inside the Whale," "The truth is that in 1917 there was nothing that a thinking and sensitive person could do, except to remain human, if possible." The narrator, we infer, had found it temporarily impossible.

The line which now reads "I am the enemy you killed, my friend," was originally "I was a German conscript and your friend." The change is an obvious improvement in being less didactic and topical, but also in another way. The irony still remains that the "enemy" was not really that, and is still followed by the implication that the Other might have lived if the narrator had maintained enough humanity to face him as an individual person. But in substituting "the enemy" for "German conscript," Owen was at once generalizing and keeping the way open for the dual level of mental and physical which he had been at such pains to establish. On one level "the enemy" is a German soldier whom the narrator killed with a bayonet. But on another level "the enemy" is just what the poem presents him as, a vision dwelling in the deep profound, an alter ego ("whatever hope is yours was my life also"), the seat of the emotions of love and laughter, grief and pity. The Other, that is, represents the narrator's unconscious, his primal self from which he has been alienated by war. Instead of retaining the hope of establishing in the future full contact with his emotions and the healing power of that primal self, the narrator (perhaps seduced by the propaganda about the Enemy) has discarded pity, the one emotion war might distill, and has at that point given up his humanity. This failure results first in spiritual death (the killing of the Other, whether as enemy or alter ego) and then in physical death (that of the narrator, who is presumably dead, though he has not been "killed").

As the Other predicts, impersonality will become the rule. But had he not been killed, that is, had the positive emotions of the unconscious not been denied entirely, after the bloody end of conflict, regeneration would have welled up from the primitive seat of life:

> "Then, when much blood had clogged their chariot-wheels
> I would go up and wash them from sweet wells,
> Even with truths that lie too deep for taint.
> I would have poured my spirit without stint
> But not on wounds; not on the cess of war.
> Foreheads of men have bled where no wounds were."

If the image of regeneration from the unconscious is not clear enough in the poem as printed, two discarded alternatives for the third line above make it clear that the wells lie in the mind:

<pre>
                     thoughts that lie
      Even the {
                     wells I sank
</pre>

In addition, in the back of Owen's *Poems* Blunden prints fragments either parallel with "Strange Meeting" "or at length interwoven with it." The first of these also makes clear the descent into the unconscious. "Let us lie down and dig ourselves in thought."

"Strange Meeting" is the product of such digging in thought. It demonstrates Owen's realization that what was of transcendent importance to the fighting man should not be his physical suffering contrasted with the comfort of civilians, but first the dehumanization of war, its ability to turn men into spiritual automatons, and second the paradoxical alternative it offered him of learning pity through involvement with suffering. This one emotion could keep alive the spark of humanity and hope which would suffice to bring regeneration to the individual, and to mankind when the slaughter finally ceased. Having dug deep into his own mind, Owen had reached the thoughts that lie too deep for taint. Of these he saw pity as the one most accessible to mankind during a war, which explains his announcement in the preface to this poems that his "subject is War, and the pity of War," and clarifies the otherwise cryptic sentence that followed, "The poetry is in the pity." In readying a book for publication, he looked forward to reaching the imaginations of his readers through poems which were the fruits of his imagination, embodiments of his consciously sought participation in an emotional synthesis with his unconscious.

—Elliott B. Gose Jr., "Digging In: An Interpretation of Wilfred Owen's 'Strange Meeting,'" *College English* 22, no. 6 (March 1961): pp. 418–19.

DOMINIC HIBBERD ON OWEN'S OTHER

[Dominic Hibberd is a writer and critic with a special interest in the literature of World War I. His works include *The First World War* (1990), *Owen the Poet* (1986), *Poetry of the Great War: An Anthology* (edited with John Onions) (1986), *Wilfred Owen* (1975), and *Wilfred Owen: The Last Year 1917–1918* (1992). In this excerpt from *Owen the Poet*, Hibberd discusses some possible interpretations of the identity of the Other in "Strange Meeting."]

The ambiguities of the poem centre on the identity of the Other. It has been common to regard him as Owen's double, an *alter ego* whose poetic creed and career are those of his author. However, until a late stage of revision, Owen thought of him as 'a German conscript', an enemy counterpart rather than a *Doppelgänger*—and not quite a counterpart, either, since Owen himself was a volunteer and had already turned away from some of the ideals which the Other adumbrates. Tailhade had warned young recruits that they would be expected to kill men whose lives had been similar to their own. Nevertheless, Owen would have been aware that encounters between a man and his other self are common in Romantic literature (they occur in Shelley and Dickens, for example). He may well have read an article by W. C. Rivers in the *Cambridge Magazine* (January 1918) which discussed Yeats's recent use of the double, relating it to literary tradition and Freud. Rivers observed that the double is sometimes represented as having the power to cast its original into hell and that in several stories, including *The Picture of Dorian Gray* (which Owen must have known), the original stabs his other self, thereby causing his own death; traditionally, meeting one's double is likely to be fatal. The event in Owen's poem cannot be reduced to a meeting between a man and his double—he had no intention of presenting war as a merely internal, psychological conflict—but neither is it concerned with the immediate divisions suggested by 'German' and 'conscript' or 'British' and 'volunteer'. The poem is larger and stranger than that. The two men are not identified, except that at first one is alive in hell and the Other is dead ('Whatever hope *is* yours, / *Was* my life also'). The meeting does seem to be fatal, however, since at the end the Other invites the poet to join him in sleep. This sleep is itself ambiguous, being death and rest yet also consciousness and torment. If the idea of the double is present at all, it may be in the mysteriously sexual element in this encounter between two men who meet, discover each other and sleep. There is a trace here of the narcissism evident in Owen's descriptions of those other sufferers in twilight, the Cultivated Rose and the casualty in 'Disabled'. The poet sees himself in the Other but the Other is an independent being.

If the many doubles which have been cited with reference to 'Strange Meeting' are not all strictly relevant, there are other literary parallels which seem convincing, including Dante's pitying recognitions of the agonised faces of spirits who have had to 'abandon hope' in hell. The tortured face and 'fixed eyes' of Owen's 'vision' have no lack of antecedents in Gothic fiction and Romantic poetry. In Landor's *Gebir,* for instance, the hero descends into a cavernous underworld and is told how the dead meeting the dead have 'with fixt eyes beheld / Fixt eyes'. Tortured, hypnotic eyes are stock Romantic properties; the Ancient Mariner, the last chapter of *Salammbô* and, above all, Keats's vision in the second *Hyperion,* provide examples which Owen knew well. In Keats's 'Lamia' the philosopher's relentless stare reveals the truth and kills delight. In *The Fall of Hyperion* the goddess of memory unveils her dying yet immortal face and unseeing eyes, thereby allowing the poet to share in her knowledge of the titanic wars of long ago and of the fallen Titans lying 'roof'd in by black rocks . . . in pain / And darkness, for no hope':

> deathwards progressing
> To no death was that visage; it had past
> The lilly and the snow; and beyond these
> I must not think now, though I saw that face. . . .

The first draft of 'Strange Meeting' mentions the whiteness of the Other's face: 'With a thousand fears his [strange, white] face was grained'. The *Hyperion* passage is also echoed in 'The Sentry', another description of seeing fixed eyes in a dug-out: 'I try not to remember these things now'. Murry said in 1919 that *The Fall of Hyperion* was undoubtedly Owen's source: the 'sombre imagination, the sombre rhythm [of 'Strange Meeting'] is that of the dying Keats . . . this poem by a boy with the certainty of death in his heart, like his great forerunner, is the most magnificent expression of the emotional significance of the war that has yet been achieved by English poetry'. Owen could have wished for no greater compliment.

—Dominic Hibberd, *Owen the Poet* (London: Macmillan, 1986): pp. 177–78.

Thematic Analysis of
"Anthem for Doomed Youth"

"Anthem for Doomed Youth" was written at Craiglockhart in September and October 1917. Sassoon helped with the revision of the poem—there were at least seven drafts—and, according to a letter Owen wrote to his mother, supplied a title as well.

"Anthem for Doomed Youth" was most likely inspired by a prefatory note to an anthology of modern poetry that mentions "the passing-bells of Death." The differences between the first draft and the last show how Owen began to reconcile his lyrical style with his opinions about the war. The poem works through a series of contrasts to suggest that the realities of war negate the values of ordinary, peaceful life; in particular, war negates Christianity.

Earlier drafts of "Anthem for Doomed Youth" contained more patriotic and sanctifying language, but Owen subsequently added elements to heighten the sense of dissonance between the solemn religious rites known during peace and the cruel parody of these ceremonies in war. The first line, for instance, shows how the experience of death, as well as our response to it, has been warped by the nature of war; in war, men suffer the senseless, anonymous death of cattle, and their death is honored merely with more fighting. In addition to the image of men being slaughtered like cattle, the poem describes the "monstrous anger of the guns," the meaningless repetition of the pattering rifles, and the "shrill, demented choirs" of the shells. By the end of the first stanza, one is left with the sense that not only does the war erase the trappings of Christianity, but religion itself is revealed to be impotent and meaningless.

The same bugles that now sound the "Last Post" for the fallen soldiers were the ones that previously called them to colors. Church and state are thus both implicated in the betrayal of the soldiers.

Owen's preoccupation with the inadequacy of traditional evaluations of the world, particularly religion, may have stemmed in part from his own experience with Christianity as a child. Growing up, he read a passage from the Bible every day, and sometimes on Sundays would rearrange his parents' sitting room to represent a church. Gathering the rest of the family into the room, the young Owen would provide them with an evening service complete with sermon. Later, while preparing for the university entrance exam, Owen served as a lay assistant to the Rev. Herbert Wigan. He gradually grew disillusioned with the conservative, evangelical religion offered by Wigan, and perhaps this early sensitivity to the limitations of formal religious activity paved the way for his later indignation at the church's support of the war.

Although Owen ultimately rejected conservative, evangelical religion, he was nevertheless continually plagued by a sense of guilt over his conflicting roles as a soldier and Christian. He wrote to his mother of his realization that "pure Christianity will not fit in with pure patriotism."

The difference between the octave and the sestet is striking. The former, which details the experience on the battlefield, lashes out at the incongruities and discrepancies between home-front rites and the degradations imposed on soldiers in battle. The sestet, which brings the reader back to the home-front, suggests that if dead soldiers cannot find immortality in the ritualized abstractions of religious ceremony, then they can still find it in the memory and affection of their families. If the religious rituals in the first eight lines have been overwhelmed by the war, here their consolatory purpose is valorized by the effect they have on the mourners. Candles, palls, and flowers, may be inadequate, but the "holy glimmers of goodbyes" in shining eyes, the "pallor of girls' brows," and the "tenderness of patient minds" offer an adequate response to suffering and death.

The differences in tone between the first and second stanzas have caused some critics to characterize the sonnet as a relapse into Owen's youthful Romanticism, an unintentional glorification of war's death. Jon Silkin, for instance, writes that "there is an ambiguity in the poem in that Owen seems to be caught in the very act of consolatory mourning he condemns in 'What passing-bells for these who die as cattle?'—a consolation that permits the war's continuation by civilian assent. . . ." Along the same lines, Geoffrey Hill has argued that the sestet ultimately fails to provide an appropriate response to the war:

> The fact that Owen employs irony in this poem cannot alter the fact that he takes thirteen lines to retreat from the position maintained by

one. If these men really do die as cattle, then all human mourning for them is a mockery, the private and the public, the inarticulate and true as much as the ostentatiously false.

Despite these criticisms, "Anthem for Doomed Youth" is a useful poem for revealing some of the important disjunctions Owen felt the war created. The poem indicates how seriously Owen took his responsibility to voice his outrage and despair on behalf of his fellow soldiers whose voices, he felt, had been silenced by rattling guns and tolling bells. ❀

Critical Views on
"Anthem for Doomed Youth"

[Philip Larkin was an eminent British poet and writer known for his use of traditional poetic devices to explore the uncomfortable and upsetting experiences of the modern age. His works include *The North Ship* (1946), *A Girl in Winter* (1947), *The Less Deceived* (1955), *The Whitsun Weddings* (1964), and *High Windows* (1974). In this 1963 review of C. Day Lewis's edition of *The Collected Poems of Wilfred Owen,* Larkin attempts to put Owen and his poetry in historical context.]

In the case of Owen, not only what he wrote but how he wrote it might fairly be called historically predictable. He was part of what Dr D. S. R. Welland calls 'the Phase of Protest', the wave of sickened indignation born of the Battle of the Somme and Passchendaele that produced the 'no annexations and no indemnities' peace agitations of 1917, and a new and shocking realism in art and literature:

> The place was rotten with dead: green clumsy legs
> High-booted, sprawled and grovelled along the saps
> And trunks, face downward, in the sucking mud
> Wallowed like trodden sandbags loosely filled;
> And naked sodden buttocks, mats of hair,
> Bulged, clotted heads slept in the plastering slime . . .

He had also been anticipated, as in these lines by Siegfried Sassoon, a writer some years his senior who since 1914 had moved independently from Dr. Welland's stage of Bardic Rhetorical ('And, fighting for our freedom, we are free') to one which Owen adopted almost immediately. The two men met in a war hospital in August 1917, where they were both nerve patients: Owen because he had just had three months in a bad sector on the Western Front, Sassoon because he had sent his Commanding Officer a letter saying: 'I believe that this war, upon which I entered as a war of defence and liberation, has now become a war of aggression and conquest'. Sassoon was already known for his war poems (or rather, anti-war poems), and Owen immediately assumed a position of admiring pupillage. They were both anxious that the war should be shown up, that the carnage, the waste, the exploitation should all be brought home to innocent noncombatants. Sassoon, whose characteristic voice was a bitter casualness ('Does it matter? —losing your legs?'), has in *Siegfried's Journey* deprecated the notion that his own example was crucial in Owen's development: he calls it 'one of those situations where imperceptible effects are obtained by people mingling their minds at a favourable moment'. At any rate, it is hard to imagine that Owen would have written 'Smile, Smile, Smile' or 'The Dead-Beat' without this coincidental and fortunate contact.

But in fact we have very little idea of how Owen developed, whether in ideas or technique: all that seems certain is that he experienced a year and a half of intense poetic activity in 1917–18 until his death seven days before the Armistice. The present editor does not follow the vaguely chronological order of Edmund Blunden's 1931 edition (from which the memoir is reprinted): he opens with a tremendous barrage of Owen's most effective pieces, leaving the early and minor poems to follow at leisure through the gap thus torn. A sonnet, '1914', is full of foreboding ('now the Winter of the World / With perishing foul darkness closes in'), but there is little to show whether Owen's view of the war changed. In 'Exposure' (presumed to date from February 1917, though Dr Welland thinks it was extensively revised later) occurs the verse:

> Since we believe not otherwise can kind
> fires burn;
> Nor ever suns smile true on child,
> or field, or fruit.
> For God's invincible spring our love is
> made afraid;
> Therefore, not loath, we lie out here;
> therefore were born;
> For love of God seems dying.

This is very much what Sassoon's bishops were saying. But in a letter written a month or so later from hospital he adopts a very different outlook:

> Already I have comprehended a light which will never filter into the dogma of any national church: namely, that one of Christ's essential commands was: Passivity at any price! Suffer dishonour and disgrace, but never resort to arms. Be bullied, be outraged, be killed, but do not

kill. It may be a chimerical and an ignominious principle, but there it is. . . . Thus you see how pure Christianity will not fit in with pure patriotism.

It was the second view that prevailed. But though Owen had in fact been religiously trained (for almost two years he was a lay assistant to a vicar in Oxfordshire), his pacifism was less a Christian principle than 'the philosophy of many soldiers', a passionate conviction that anything is better than war and its annihilations:

> O Life, Life, let me breathe—a dug-out rat!
> Not worse than ours the existences rats lead—
> Nosing along at night down some safe rut,
> They find a shell-proof home before they rot,
> Dead men many envy living mites in cheese . . .

There could hardly be any plainer statement that what is terrible about war is the premature death ('there was a quaking / Of the aborted life within him leaping') or disablement it brings:

> 'Strange friend', I said, 'here is no cause to mourn'.
> 'None', said that other, 'save the undone years. . .'.

The conviction was to permeate the entire national consciousness during the next twenty years; it reached forward to Baldwin's refusal to re-arm, Dick Sheppard and the Peace Pledge Union, and Chamberlain flying to Berchtesgaden. 'It is Owen, I believe', writes Mr C. Day Lewis in his introduction, 'whose poetry came home deepest to members of my generation, so that we could never again think of war as anything but a vile, if necessary, evil'. That 'if necessary', which would not have been there before 1939, shows that on the whole the implications of Owen's poems have been found unacceptable. We do not honour him the less for this, but it strengthens the historical limitations that attend his work.

—Philip Larkin, "The War Poet" (review of *The Collected Poems of Wilfred Owen*), *The Listener* (10 October 1963): p. 561.

[Siegfried Sassoon was a poet and writer best known for the poetry and memoirs that stemmed from his experiences of World War I. In this excerpt from his diary, Sassoon recalls meeting fellow poet Wilfred Owen for the first time at Craiglockhart Hospital, where they were both recovering from shell-shock.]

⟨. . .⟩ It amuses me to remember that, when I had resumed my ruminative club polishing, I wondered whether his poems were any good! He had seemed an interesting little chap but had not struck me as remarkable. In fact my first view of him was as a rather ordinary young man, perceptibly provincial, though unobtrusively ardent in his responses to my lordly dictums about poetry. Owing to my habit of avoiding people's faces while talking, I had not observed him closely. Anyhow, it was pleasant to have discovered that there was another poet in the hospital and that he happened to be an admirer of my work. For him on the other hand, the visit to my room—as he subsequently assured me—had been momentous. It had taken him two whole weeks, he said, to muster up enough courage to approach me with his request. I must add that, in a letter to his mother—shown me many years afterwards—he reported me as talking badly. "He accords a slurred suggestion of words only. . . . The last thing he said to me was 'Sweat your guts out writing poetry.' He also warned me against early publishing. He is himself thirty. Looks under twenty-five." This must have been written a few days later, after he had diffidently shown me a selection of his verse, for he describes me—I am thankful to say—as "applauding some of it long and fervently" and pronouncing one of his recent lyrics ("Song of Songs") "perfect work, absolutely charming," and asking him to copy it for me. I record my thankfulness, because I have an uncomfortable suspicion that I was a bit slow in recognizing the exceptional quality of his poetic gift. Manuscript poems can be deceptive when handed to one like school exercises to be blue-penciled, especially when one has played thirty-six holes of golf and consumed a stodgy hospital dinner. I was sometimes a little severe on what he showed me, censuring the over-luscious writing in his immature pieces, and putting my finger on "She dreams of golden gardens and sweet glooms" as an example. But it was the emotional element, even more than its verbal expression, which seemed to need refinement. There was an almost embarrassing sweetness in the sentiment of some of his work, though it showed skill in rich and melodious combinations of words. This weakness, as hardly requires pointing out, he was progressively discarding during the last year of his life. In his masterpiece "Strange Meeting" he left us the finest elegy written by a soldier of that period and the conclusive testimony of his power and originality. It was, however, not until some time in October, when he brought me his splendidly constructed sonnet "Anthem for Doomed Youth," that it dawned on me that my little friend was much more than the promising minor poet I had hitherto adjudged him to be. I now realized that his verse, with its sumptuous epithets and large-scale imagery, its noble naturalness and depth of meaning, had impressive affinities with Keats, whom he took as his supreme exemplar. This new sonnet was a revelation. I suggested one or two slight alterations; but it confronted me with classic and imaginative serenity. After assuring him of its excellence I told him that I would do my best to get it published in *The Nation*. This gratified him greatly. Neither of us could have been expected to foresee that it would some day be added to Palgrave's *Golden Treasury*.

It has been loosely assumed and stated that Wilfred modelled his war poetry on mine. My only claimable influence was that I stimulated him towards writing with compassionate and challenging realism. His printed letters are evidence that the impulse was already strong in him before he had met me. The manuscript of one of his most dynamically descriptive war poems, "Exposure," is dated February 1917, and proves that he had already found an authentic utterance of his own. (For some reason, he withheld this poem from me while we were together.) Up to a point my admonitions were helpful. My encouragement was opportune, and can claim to have given him a lively incentive during his rapid advance to self-revelation. Meanwhile I seem to hear him laughingly implore me to relax these expository generalizations and recover some of the luminous animation of our intimacy. How about any indirect influence on him? he inquires in his calm velvety voice. Have I forgotten our eager discussion of contemporary poets and the technical dodges which we were ourselves devising? Have I forgotten the simplifying suggestions which emanated from my unsophisticated poetic method? (For my technique was almost elementary compared with his innovating experiments.) Wasn't it after he got to know me that he first began to risk using the colloquialisms which were at that time so frequent in my verses? And didn't I lend him Barbusse's *Le Feu*, which set him alight as no other war book had done? It was indeed one of those situations where imperceptible effects are obtained by people mingling their minds at a favourable moment. Turning the pages of Wilfred's *Poems*, I am glad to think that there may have been occasions when some freely improvised remark of mine sent him away with a fruitful idea. And my humanized reportings of front-line episodes may have contributed something to his controlled vision of what he had seen for himself. Of his own period of active service he seldom spoke. I was careful to avoid questioning him about the experiences which had caused his nervous breakdown, and was only vaguely aware of what he had been through in the St. Quentin sector and elsewhere. Fourteen years later, when reading the letters quoted by Edmund Blunden in his finally authoritative *Memoir*, I discovered that Wilfred had endured worse things than I had realized from the little he told me. On arriving at the Western Front he had immediately encountered abominable conditions of winter weather and attrition warfare. But of this he merely remarked to me that he wished he'd had my luck in being inured to the beastly business by gradual stages. His thick dark hair was already touched with white above the ears.

—Siegfried Sassoon, *Siegfried's Journey 1916–1920* (New York: The Viking Press, 1946): pp. 87–91.

JON SILKIN ON OWEN AND CONSOLATION IN "ANTHEM FOR DOOMED YOUTH"

[Jon Silkin is a respected poet perhaps best known for his writings on other poets. His works include *The Peaceable Kingdom* (1954), *Isaac Rosenberg, 1890–1918: A Catalogue of an Exhibition Held at Leeds University* (1959), with Maurice de Sausmarez, *Out of Battle: The Poetry of the Great War* (1972), *The Penguin Book of First World War Poetry* (editor and author of introduction) (1979), and *The Penguin Book of First World War Prose* (editor, with Jon Glover) (1989). Silkin is also co-editor of *Stand*, a quarterly review of the arts, and a contributor to numerous literary publications. In this excerpt from the second edition of *Out of Battle: The Poetry of the Great War,* Silkin looks at Owen's ambivalent approach to the search for consolation in "Anthem for Doomed Youth."]

Owen was discharged from Craiglockhart in November 1917 and posted then to the Northern Cavalry Barracks, Scarborough. In the spring and early summer of 1918 he worked as an instructor where, as Johnston observes, he felt 'his conflicting roles of leader and betrayer': 'For 14 hours yesterday I was at work—teaching Christ to lift his cross by numbers'. At the end of August he returned to his old battalion in France. Blunden records that C. K. Scott-Moncrieff, 'then at the War Office, endeavoured to find some post for Owen which would mean that he would be kept in England'. And on 21 May Owen wrote that, although it seemed he had some opportunity 'of becoming Instructing Staff Officer to a Cadet Battalion[,] I would *rather* work in the War Office itself, and that seems not impossible either. Really I would *like most* to go to Egypt or Italy, but that is not entertained by Scott-Moncrieff.' But none of these possibilities occurred and in July, preparing for the Western Front, he wrote, 'Now must I throw my little candle on [Sassoon's] torch and go out again' and 'I am glad. That is I am much gladder to be going out again than afraid. I shall be better able to cry my outcry, playing my part.' I imagine that Owen's prior reluctance to return was partly caused by the anxiety he must surely have felt that the war might cut short his realizing his full potential as a poet; and, if this is so, it is not completely consonant which his brother's comment on the poet's attitudes subsequent to his enlistment: 'Wilfred having given himself that first year to make his own decision was content with [its] rightness . . . he never wavered in this and never looked back with regret.' Yet such natural dismay as returning to the front must have produced, is turned to remarkable account in 'able to cry my outcry, playing my part'. Owen was not unaware of the double-edgedness of the situation; from the front he wrote to Sassoon on 22 September: 'You said it would be a good thing for my poetry if I went back. That is my consolation for feeling a fool. This is what shells scream at me every time: Haven't you got the wits to keep out of this?' But in all this ambiguity he is determined that his poetry shall plead for those who suffer and are inarticulate—to those who are ignorant of, or apathetic to, this suffering.

'Anthem for Doomed Youth' makes this plea by comparing the soldiers' peremptory treatment with that which cattle receive prior to their slaughter. The consolatory and decorous ceremonies of religious and institutional mourning contrast with the brutal nature of their deaths. Yet there is ambiguity in the poem in that Owen seems to be caught in the very act of consolatory mourning he condemns in 'What passing-bells for these who die as cattle?'—a consolation that permits the war's continuation by civilian assent, and which is found ambiguously in the last line of the octet: 'And bugles calling for them from sad shires.' Is 'sad shires' ironic, or consolatory (for Benjamin Britten in the *War Requiem* the line has no ambiguity; the interpretive music is sweetly elegiac). Geoffrey Hill, in a review of Keith Douglas's *Selected Poems,* writes: 'The fact that Owen employs irony in this poem cannot alter the fact that he takes thirteen lines to retreat from the position maintained by [the first].' The first line of the sestet may question what kind of cheer may be wished the embarking soldiers, but 'candle', already in an antique mode, steadily leads to pastoral elegy that so falsifies their actual deaths:

> Their flowers the tenderness of patient minds,
> And each slow dusk a drawing-down of blinds.

The sorrowing patient minds of the women in mourning are no different from the sorrowful religious consolation we have been taught to accept in exchange for human lives, and the sanctified nature of the soldiers' deaths found in grieving 'shires' and 'flowers' excludes the horror of war as effectively as if Owen had been propagandizing for the war. The pun of 'pallor' with 'pall' is consonant with this kind of elegizing, but he misses the perhaps better pun more consonant with his later poems in 'pall' 'appal'. Peter Dale has also remarked on the weakness of the poem which 'sets up memory as an equalizer of the suffering on the field and in the home and makes some sort of compensation out of it'.

—Jon Silkin, *Out of Battle: The Poetry of the Great War* (London: Macmillian, 1998): pp. 209–11.

DOMINIC HIBBERD ON OWEN'S ROMANTIC INHERITANCE

[In this selection, Hibberd argues that "Anthem for Doomed Youth," a poem that has been criticized for glorifying death in war, reflects the tension in Owen's writing between his earlier, more lyrical and Romantic style and the influence of Sassoon's realist approach to writing about the war.]

'Anthem for Doomed Youth' was completed by 25 September after advice from Sassoon, who recognised for the first time that Owen's talent was out of the ordinary. The differences between the first draft and the last (there were at least seven drafts) show how Owen began to bring his lyrical writing into step with his opinions about the war. The result was a sonorous but rather confused poem; there was still much to get straight, but he had made a start:

> What passing-bells for these who die as cattle?
>   —Only the monstrous anger of the guns.
>   Only the stuttering rifles' rapid rattle
> Can patter out their hasty orisons.
> No mockeries now for them; no prayer nor bells;
>   Nor any voice of mourning save the choirs,—
> The shrill, demented choirs of wailing shells;
>   And bugles calling for them from sad shires.
>
> What candles may be held to speed them all?
>   Not in the hands of boys but in their eyes
> Shall shine the holy glimmers of good-byes.
>   The pallor of girls' brows shall be their pall;
> Their flowers the tenderness of patient minds,
> And each slow dusk a drawing-down of blinds.

This sonnet has come in for some sharp criticism as a relapse into Owen's youthful Romanticism and as an unintentional glorification of death in war. The first point seems to me misleading. The poem's language is certainly Keatsian ('Then in a *wail*ful *choir* the small gnats *mourn*') but the allusions are meant to be noticed, revealing the battlefield as a demented parody of the Romantic landscape. The second point, that 'Anthem' has a sanctifying effect on its subject, is more accurate, except that the first draft shows that originally this effect was by no means unintended. The draft begins by asking, 'What minute bells for these who die so fast?' Answer: 'Only the monstrous/solemn anger of our guns'. The only possible response to the slaughter (of British troops) is that 'our' guns should hurl angry 'insults' at the enemy. The poet explains his function, which is to arouse grief and remembrance, by saying that 'I will light' the candles which will shine in boys' eyes (meaning that his poems will produce tears in the eyes of soldiers' sons or younger brothers). The funeral ceremonies will not be church services, since battle conditions prevent such things, but the majestic 'requiem' of British artillery in France and the sadness of bereaved families in England. Whether such rites are adequate or not, the poem does not say; they are the only possible ones, that is all.

Sassoon would have seen the first draft's shortcomings at once. Even if Owen did not mean it to be a statement in support of the British war effort, it could be used in that way. It was uncomfortably close to popular war poems such as Laurence Binyon's 'For the Fallen' or Beatrix Brice's 'To the Vanguard'. So Sassoon cancelled 'solemn' in favour of 'monstrous' and changed 'our guns' and 'majestic insults' to 'the guns' and 'blind insolence'. Owen followed these pointers in subsequent drafts, removing the anti-German and sanctifying elements from the octave by making shells 'demented', introducing the 'patter' of rifles (the word derives from the meaningless repetition of paternosters) and describing doomed youth as 'cattle' for whom any rites would be 'mockeries'. These changes do not fully conceal the tone of the first draft, but they might have been enough if the sestet had been different. If Sassoon sensed that the last six lines were unsatisfactory, he would not have known Owen well enough to see what was wrong. The difficult transition from battlefields to home is admirably managed by means of bugles, which were familiar in both places (memorial services in 'sad shires' often ended with a bugle call). But the strongest objection to 'Anthem' is that its sestet betrays Owen's hard-won maturity by slipping back into the nostalgia that he had expressed in 'A New Heaven' before he had seen the trenches. The sestets of both sonnets propose that dead soldiers can find immortality in the memory and affection of their families. The first draft of 'Anthem' even says that the men's wreaths will be 'Women's wide-spread arms', but after Beaumont Hamel Owen had said in 'Happiness' that he had gone *beyond* 'the scope / Of mother-arms' (or of 'the wide arms of trees'). It is not difficult to sense the presence of Colin, Mary and Mrs Owen among the weeping boys, pale girls and patient minds in the final sestet of 'Anthem', but there could be no return even in death. The hardest thing of all for a soldier to accept was that even his own family would not understand or remember; Owen was to come to terms with this after Craiglockhart.

It is unjust to treat 'Anthem' as a 'late' poem on a level with 'Strange Meeting' or 'Insensibility', as some critics have done. It should be seen as Owen's first attempt to bring his own style into line with the views he was learning from Sassoon. Unlike his more obviously Sassoonish poems, 'Anthem' draws extensively on what he had heard and read in Bordeaux as a way of resisting his friend's overwhelming stylistic influence. The elegiac tone, elaborate sound-patterns and elegant metaphors are more Tailhadesque than Sassoonish. Phrases in the first draft—'solemn', '[priest-words] requiem of their [burials]', 'choristers and holy music', 'voice of mourning', 'many [candles shine]'—seem to derive from his account of a French funeral service in 1914:

> The gloom, the incense, the draperies, the shine of many candles, the images and ornaments, were what may be got anywhere in England; but the solemn voices of the priests was what I had never heard before. The melancholy of a bass voice, mourning, now alone, now in company with other voices or with music, was altogether fine; as fine as the Nightingale—(bird or poem).

—Dominic Hibberd, *Owen the Poet* (London: Macmillian, 1998): pp. 109–112.

DAVID DAICHES ON OWEN AND LANGUAGE

[David Daiches is a British literary critic known for his several studies of leading English literary figures. He has written on writers as varied as Virginia Woolf, Robert Burns, Willa Cather, Robert Louis Stevenson, Walt Whitman, and John Milton. In this excerpt from his 1936 work *New Literary Values: Studies in Modern Literature,* Daiches suggests that Owen earned a place of his own in the history of English poetry by being able to situate his understanding of the war within a larger context of human experience.]

We may well ask what a poet can do in the face of such a devastating experience as modern warfare. What, at least, should he try to do? Is it his duty to denounce war in stirring rhetoric, or to glorify his cause and his country, or to describe what he sees, or to preach a point of view? There have been poets who have done all these things. But Wilfred Owen did very much more. He came to the war with an intense poetic sensibility, a generous and understanding nature, and an ability to penetrate to the inner reality of the experience in the midst of which he found himself. "Inner reality" is a vague term, but its definition is implied in Owen's poetry. It refers to an ability to relate these particular facts to the rest of human experience, to the life of men and woman in cities and fields, to see war in its relation to all this, to appreciate just what this activity meant—what it meant as a whole and what particular aspects of it meant—in a world which was already old before the war, where happiness and suffering were no new phenomena, where men had lived diversely and foolishly and richly and gone about their occupations and were to do so again when all this was over. Owen never forgot what normal human activity was like, and always had a clear sense of its relation to the abnormal activity of war. ⟨. . .⟩

What Owen's place in the development of English poetry might have been can only be a matter of conjecture, and conjecture of this kind is never very profitable. But it is enough to judge him by what he did accomplish, leaving aside all hypothetical questions of what he might have done. His achievement was very real. Out of his experiences in the war he fashioned poetry which expresses in rich and cogent English some of the most fundamental aspects of human thought and emotion. Amid all the horror that he encountered he preserved unscathed his sense of values and his power of intense observation and penetration, never allowing his judgment to be warped by personal bitterness or his powers of expression to be weakened through fear or prejudice. His poetry serves a double function. It stands as a lasting exposure of the pity and futility of war, and at the same time it illumines significant channels of human experience that belong to no one time and place. His poetry, he said, was not "about deeds, or lands, nor anything about glory, honour, might, majesty, dominion, or power, except War." It is because he kept those terribly clear eyes of his constantly on the object that, in writing of war, he wrote at the same time a commentary on much more than war. By limiting his aim, with an honesty of purpose rare among poets, he enlarged his achievement.

No estimate of Owen is complete without a reference to his genuine nobility of character, brought out so well in Mr. Blunden's memoir with its numerous quotations from his letters. The quality is apparent, too, in his poetry—so much so, indeed, that the critic comes to a discussion of Owen's poetry with a humility not often associated with critical activity. We cannot help feeling that Owen the man was greater than the poet and that his early death involved what we may call a loss to society as great as the loss to poetry. Yet in lamenting what we lost, let us not forget what we have gained. The poetry of Wilfred Owen, slight though it is in bulk, is a rich contribution to English literature. The farther back the war years recede into the past the more clearly he stands out above the mass of war poets.

—David Daiches, *New Literary Values: Studies in Modern Literature* (London: Oliver and Boyd, 1936): pp. 61, 66–67.

Thematic Analysis of
"Futility"

Owen wrote "Futility" sometime in May 1918, and it first appeared on June 15, 1918 in *The Nation,* along with the poem "Hospital Barge." In Owen's lists of poems for publication, these two poems are placed next to each other, and the descriptive subheading for both poems is "Grief." Jon Silkin has written that "Futility" "hovers between outrage and elegy." Here, in one of Owen's last and finest poems, he literally dissects the aftermath of war, turning to an actual piece of the human wreckage.

The poem stays away from any overt mention of the war, focusing rather on the response to death and the attempt to understand its meaning. The body of a dying soldier is placed in the sun, the source of warmth and life in pre-war days: "Gently its touch awoke him once, / At home, whispering of fields half-sown." The language in this stanza conveys the untroubled, easy memory of pre-war days; the "kind" sun's gentle touch and the whispering fields are like a dreamy lullaby that offers the promise of security and regeneration. While in many of his poems Owen goes to great lengths to empha-size the brutality and violence of death, here in this first stanza the implied death of the soldier is juxtaposed to pre-war sleeping.

But the sun is unable to wake the soldier, to restore life to him. From this point in the poem, the natural processes evoked with such promise in the first few lines become undone. The harmony in which humanity and nature once lived has been destroyed. The gentle, hopeful tone of the first stanza gives way to a growing pitch of disillusionment in the second stanza; the restorative power of the sun suffers ironic depreciation because it cannot restore the life it helped to form.

Continuing with the image of the natural cycle, Owen reminds the reader of how the sun coaxes life from seeds and crops. Yet the ben-efit of this cycle is undermined by the sun's inability to raise this dead man. "O what made fatuous sunbeams toil / To break earth's sleep at all?" the poet queries, suggesting that this waste of life is such that it would have been better had the process not even begun. The poet's bitterness and his sense of betrayal stem from the loss of his faith in the natural processes, which, like religion, has not been able to withstand the war. The breakdown of the cycle of life represents the triumph of chaos.

"Futility" has been singled out for the remarkable subtlety of its rhyming patterns that reflect a muted, minor tone. Owen shows how far he has come in mastering his poetic technique, relying on not the strong sounds of consonant clusters and combinations but the less obtrusive melody of vowel cadences, rhythm, and an utter simplicity of diction. The regular rhyme patterns of the stanzas mingle true and half-rhyme. In the second stanza, the vowels lengthen, and the rhythm is slowed by a succession of halting adjectival phrases: "Are limbs, so dear-achieved, are sides / Full-nerved—still warm—too hard to stir?" These syntactically fragmented lines suggest a reluctance or hesitancy to fully accept the implications of this wasteful death.

Some critics have seen "Futility" as a pointed rebuttal of the 19th-century view of the meaning of human life, others, as a rebuttal of the elegiac mode itself. The poem contains all the usual themes of elegy—a death, a sympathetically barren landscape, the image of wasted youth, the invocation of a divine or natural power. And yet in "Futility," these components emerge as fragments of a now broken form. Although the meditative, quiet mood of much of the poem raises the reader's expectations that the poem is an elegy that will end with suitably elegiac resignation, it builds instead toward the satirical word "fatuous," thus ending in a spirit of protest and disgust: "O what made fatuous sunbeams toil / To break earth's sleep at all?"

The final lines argue with resignation itself, for the poet's voice refuses to be comforted. Owen's loss of faith in nature is thus mirrored in his rejection of the conventions of elegy. The result, as one critic has observed, is "a poetic transformation of battlefield death, death particular and individual, into death as the absurd and ultimate denial of the value of life." ❀

Critical Views on
"Futility"

[C. Day Lewis was the late Poet Laureate of England, appointed in 1968. Author of *A Hope for Poetry* (1934), *A Time to Dance and Other Poems* (1935), and *Noah and the Waters* (1936), among other works, Lewis was once considered a poet of revolution, inextricably linked with the avant-garde Oxford poets of the 1930s, W. H. Auden, Stephen Spender, and Louis MacNeice. In this selection from his introduction to *The Collected Poems of Wilfred Owen*, Lewis argues that, while lacking the kind of emotional intensity of his later poems, Owen's earliest reactions to the war already revealed hints of the sharp sense of observation and interest in other people that would characterize the best of his later work.]

When war broke out, Wilfred Owen, a provincial himself, was living the life of a cultivated, French provincial society. He was now twenty-one—unsophisticated, inexperienced, still only intermittently sure of his vocation, but ardent and sensuous at the core. For a month or two, the war hardly touched him or the social circle in which he lived. His own attitude towards it was not that of a "swimmer into cleanness leaping": it was nearer to that of certain Bloomsbury figures who resented the war as an unseemly disturbance of the private life; but with this difference—that Owen's protest was raw, violent, naïf, deadly serious:

> *I feel my own life all the more precious and more dear in the presence of this deflowering of Europe. While it is true that the guns will effect a little useful weeding, I am furious with chagrin to think that the Minds, which were to have excelled the civilization of two thousand years, are being annihilated—and bodies, the product of aeons of Natural Selection, melted down to pay for political statues.*
>
> Letter of August 28th, 1914.

A month later, Owen was for the first time brought up hard against the facts of war. The experience, since he had a poet's inner toughness, proved salutary rather than traumatic. He visited a hospital in Bordeaux at which casualties had just arrived from the front—a hospital grievously ill prepared for such an emergency, with an inadequate water-supply, where he witnessed operations being performed without anaesthetics. In a letter of September 23 to his brother Harold, he wrote:

> One poor devil had his shin-bone crushed by a gun-carriage wheel, and the doctor had to twist it about and push it like a piston to get out the pus . . . I deliberately tell you all this to educate you to the actualities of war.

The tone is ruthless and a little self-important; but Owen was a very young man, and young men do labour to educate their families. But there is a sharpness in the observation which comes like a premonition of the unrelenting factual truthfulness we find in Owen's war poems: he wanted to shock, but never for the mere sake of shocking.

In general, his letters of the Bordeaux period show a greater interest in other human beings, and a considerable talent for sketching their externals, but no deep perception of their natures, nor any desire to see deep into them. He was still egocentric, as a young poet must be; still repeating his "need for study, intellectual training"; still oscillating between confidence and self-distrust over his vocation—on the one hand, "I seem without a footing on life; but I have one . . . I was a boy when I first realized that the fullest life liveable was a Poet's" (letter of February 6th, 1915); on the other hand, "all last year and longer I have read no poetry, nor thought poetically" (letter of February 18th, 1915). At the beginning of 1915 Owen was seriously considering whether he should take up an opening in business. He seems to have had no thoughts yet of enlisting: in any case he was bound by his contract with the Legers to stay in France till the end of the summer. It was not till June 15th that he first stated his intention of joining up as soon as his tutorial engagement was over, and there is no indication in his letters home that he had felt any conflict or compunction about remaining a civilian.

He came home in August or September, was accepted for the Army in October, and trained with the Artists' Rifles. On June 4th, 1916, he was commissioned in the Manchester Regiment. His early training took place in London, where he visited the Poetry Bookshop—

Harold Monro was "very struck" by some sonnets of Owen's, and "told me what was fresh and clever, and what was second-hand and banal; and what Keatsian and what 'modern,'" (letter of March 5th, 1916). Military training he found, as most 'temporary' soldiers find it, both arduous and tedious; apart from the discipline it inculcated, it was inevitably a playing-at-soldiers which could be only the sketchiest preparation for the realities of active service. In August, Owen contemplated a transfer to the Royal Flying Corps: "Flying is the only active profession I could ever continue with enthusiasm after the War." But he was too useful an infantry officer to release, and at the end of the year he received his orders to go out to France.

—C. Day Lewis, ed., *The Collected Poems of Wilfred Owen* (New York: New Directions, 1963): pp. 19–21.

GERTRUDE M. WHITE ON WAR AS A VIOLATION OF NATURE

[Gertrude White is a frequent contributor to literature and literary journals, including *Walt Whitman Review, Sewanee Review,* and *Criticism.* With Joan Rosen, she is the author of *A Moment's Monument: The Development of the Sonnet* (1972), and she is currently conducting research on Victorian and early 20th-century poetry. In her 1969 *Wilfred Owen,* White analyzes Owen's treatment of war as a violation of nature.]

The theme of war as a violation of nature and of natural processes is treated in several of Owen's finest poems. These tend to be less factual than imaginative or visionary interpretations of fact, and are usually built up of contrasts and comparisons which make this reversal of values vivid and explicit. "Asleep" makes its central point in one swift and striking image: the death of a soldier while asleep is described; the actual act of his dying, as well as the fact of his death. This act is presented in terms of unnatural childbirth: the soldier's body, which has been possessed of life as a woman's body is possessed of her unborn child, is delivered, as it were, of life by the bullet that kills him, as the woman might be delivered of her child by abortion. The result in both cases is unnatural death by violent interference with creative processes. War is an offense against the natural order; and in the final image of the stanza the soldier's blood, like a live creature, creeps out to investigate the intrusion of this alien violence.

"Futility," as perfect a poem as Owen ever wrote, makes the same point but in a much larger perspective. It is woven of a whole series of correspondences and antitheses: present and past, man and Nature, purposeful endeavor and futility, creation and destruction. The focus of the poem is less on the particular fact of the soldier's death than on the implication of the fact for all the cosmos. In this, too, it is akin to "Asleep," the final thrust of which is that the living who must continue to take part in such senseless violence are more to be pitied than the dead.

"Futility" opens with the present reality—the dead soldier in the snow of France—and in a mood of what sounds like controlled hope, with the speaker's command, "Move him into the sun." The sun, symbol of life and light, of the creative powers of the universe, has always awakened the youth to his task of sowing the seeds of new life. Long before his birth, the sun summoned the cold earth to life, mothering all things born. Only yesterday the youth himself was "dear-achieved," wakened to life by the creative love of man and woman, the crown and justification of the whole long process of evolution. Now that which life had toiled to bring to birth lies dead in battle, creator turned destroyer and himself destroyed: and his death makes hideous mockery of all creation: "dear-achieved" is contrasted in the penultimate line with the master stroke, "fatuous": "O what made fatuous sunbeams toil / To break earth's sleep at all?" But it is man's fatuity that has reversed the order of nature and blasphemed against the lord of life, and the lamentation of the living is less for the dead man, or for themselves personally, than for the futility of all creation in the face of war.

Implicit in many of Owen's poems is the sense of a mysterious bond between men and Nature. In violating their own human nature, in reversing by violence the natural order, men alienate themselves from Nature herself. Their dehumanization is shown often in terms of this alienation. The unnaturalness of war is reflected in their view of natural phenomena; Nature herself is affected by and echoes their violence; and men in battle or dying of wounds console themselves with dreams of another, kinder Nature with which once they were in tune and which they may again rejoin in death.

—Gertrude M. White, *Wilfred Owen* (New York: Twayne Publishers, 1969): pp. 61–62.

ARTHUR E. LANE ON "FUTILITY"

[Arthur E. Lane is professor of English at California State University, Northridge, and a poet whose works include *An Adequate Response: The War Poetry of Wilfred Owen and Siegfried Sassoon* (1972), *Dancing in the Dark* (poems) (1976), and *Handing Over* (poems) (1979). In this selection from *An Adequate Response,* Lane looks at "Futility" as an example of Owen's ability to transform his war experience into poetry.]

Owen's artistic control over the elements of hope, pathos, and despair is fully evident in this poem. By skirting the edge of sentimentality in "If anything might rouse him now / The kind old sun will know," he conveys grief sharpening to despair: a grief suddenly aware of the limits of sanity, and facing madness in order to subdue it. The outlet which the grief takes—the three questions—is a release justifiable both artistically and psychologically. Though the questions are asked in despair, there is in the last one a hint of the cathartic anger which indicates a return to bitter rationality.

The poem contains no reference to the manner of the soldier's death; indeed, it is only the totality of the poem which confirms the fact of death. Initially, there is an ambiguity permitted which is sufficient to draw the reader into momentarily entertaining the hopes of the speaker. Perhaps, after all, the man is only wounded, or sick, and would welcome the chance of lying in the sunlight. With the last two lines of the first stanza, however, the reader begins to sense the desperateness of what is happening, he has been misled into hope through the quality of the speaker's despair.

This despair, this hope, comes close to madness in the childlike simplicity of the appeal "Think how it wakes the seeds," a reference to an organic world whose values and processes, basic as they are, have become suddenly and terribly irrelevant. The speaker *knows* that the soldier is dead; it is some indication of Owen's sureness of touch that the line carries pathos rather than morbidity in its reversion to man's most primitive ideas about the source of life. The following line, separated by a dash, diverts this movement somewhat; its imagery is more conventionally mature, more assimilable as metaphor. But the pause is brief. The succeeding two lines are syntactically fragmented in a way which recalls the analogous scene from *King Lear,* the grieving king crouched over the body of his daughter: "Do you see this? Look on her, look, her lips / Look there, look there!"

The last three lines modulate the pain into anger—humanity asserting itself in the face of intolerable odds. The poem as a whole is just such a gesture of assertion, transcending its subject in the act of revealing it, making experience into art. There are many factors simultaneously at work to this end: the contrast between the emotionally neutral command which opens the first stanza and the corresponding line in the second stanza, the pathos of the second appearance of the word, "clay"; the inescapable moral significance of the epithet in "what mad fatuous sunbeams toil . . . ," the tension induced by juxtaposing half-rhyme with full rhyme—these and other elements combine and recombine to create a poetic transformation of battlefield death, death particular and individual, into death as the absurd and ultimate denial of the value of life.

—Arthur E. Lane, *An Adequate Response: The War Poetry of Wilfred Owen and Siegfried Sassoon* (Detroit: Wayne State University Press, 1972): pp. 146–47.

D. S. R. Welland on Owen's Use of Half-Rhyme

[D. S. R. Welland is a noted critic and professor of American literature at Victoria University of Manchester. His work includes *Wilfred Owen: A Critical Study* (1960), *Arthu*r

Miller (1961), and *Mark Twain in England* (1978); he is also a frequent reviewer for the *Times Literary Supplement* and other periodicals. In this selection from *Wilfred Owen: A Critical Study,* Welland offers a detailed analysis of Owen's use of half-rhyme, arguing that this poetic device enabled the poet to express the sense of frustration and hopelessness that that was the hallmark of his poetry.]

One major influence that Owen exerted on the technique of English verse is, of course, his development of half-rhyme. Reviewing the 1920 edition of the poems in the *Anthenæum* (10 December 1920) Edmund Blunden foresaw that 'the discovery of final assonances in place of rhyme may mark a new age in poetry', and certainly lyric poetry since then has made such extensive use of this device (known variously as half-rhyme, para-rhyme, or vowel dissonance) that it has become a characteristic of modern verse. The principle of it is familiar enough: instead of changing the initial consonant while retaining the vowel sound as rhyme does (cold/bold), the consonantal framework is retained and the vowel changed (cold/called/killed/curled). This is half-rhyme in its strictest form and as Owen regularly uses it, but it is, of course, not something that he invented. It occurs in proverbial expressions: 'Every bullet has its billet' or 'Many a mickle makes a muckle'. It is with us in the nursery in such a phrase as 'the man in the moon' or in the rhyme of the unfortunate Dr Foster who 'stepped in a puddle right up to his middle', and its frequency in such hyphenated popular formations as 'ship-shape', 'tip-top', riff-raff', 'dilly-dally', 'flip-flap', 'clip-clop', 'tittle-tattle' and so on is ample evidence of its attractiveness to the English ear. ⟨. . .⟩

It is no coincidence that of the fourteen complete poems in which he uses half-rhyme thirteen should have been written in the last twenty months of his life and of those only two ("Songs of Songs' and 'The Roads Also') should be unconnected with war. These poems where he was 'not concerned with Poetry' were the ideal testing ground for this new medium which offered so happy a compromise between the ordered neatness of rhyme and the shapelessness into which unrhymed verse can so easily lapse. He would be less hesitant about experimenting in those poems because in so many of them pure rhyme would have detracted from that impression of easy, unpretentious, colloquial speech at which he aimed whereas half-rhyme, giving a less 'poetic' effect, would suit the rugged ordinariness of idiom and contribute to the naturalistic movement of the verse in such dramatic monologues as 'A Terre'. To praise the unobtrusiveness of half-rhyme may be to invite the question 'Would not blank verse have been equally effective?' One of the best answers to this—and certainly the earliest—was given by John Middleton Murry reviewing the 1920 edition in *The Anthenæum* of 19 February 1921 and speaking particularly of 'Strange Meeting':

> I believe that the reader who comes fresh to this poem does not immediately observe the assonant endings. At first he feels only that the blank verse has a mournful, impressive, even oppressive quality of its own; that the poem has a forged unity, a welded and inexorable massiveness. The emotions with which it is charged cannot be escaped; the meaning of the words and the beat of the sounds have the same indivisible message. The tone is single, low, muffled, subterranean. The reader looks again and discovers the technical secret; but if he regards it then as an amazing technical innovation, he is in danger of falsifying his own reaction to the poem. These assonant endings are indeed the discovery of a genius; but in a truer sense the poet's emotion discovered them for itself. They are a dark and natural flowering of this, and only this, emotion. You cannot imagine them used for any other purpose save Owen's, or by any other hand save his. They are the very modulation of his voice; you are in the presence of that rare achievement, a true poetic style.

There, of course, is the importance of Owen's half-rhyme. That Romains, Graves and Scott Moncrieff had made similar experiments suggests an awareness that this reflected better than rhyme the disintegration of values in the world around them, but for Owen it also met a more compelling, inner need. It offered a unique and perfect expression to that diffidence and lack of self-confidence that all who knew him record, and at the same time it coincided with the hesitant sense of frustration that his poetry had to communicate. It is in this way that 'the poet's emotion discovered' these assonances 'for itself' as Middleton Murry claimed, and when Murry hears in them 'the very modulation of his voice' he testifies not only to the individuality of Owen's verse but also to its dramatic quality. Half-rhyme is right for this poetry because its note of haunting uneasiness, of frustration and melancholy, accords perfectly with the theme and the mood. The pity which is in the poetry is the more emphatically brought out by it. It is not merely a matter of subconscious disappointment caused to the reader by refusing the rhyme his ear expects, while at the same time reminding him that he was expecting it; that enters into it, but the total appeal is more subtle.

—D. S. R. Welland, *Wilfred Owen: A Critical Study* (London: Chatto and Windus, 1960): pp. 104, 118–20.

Biography of
Isaac Rosenberg

Isaac Rosenberg (1890–1918) was born in Bristol, the son of Barnett Rosenberg, a Lithuanian Jew, and Chasa Davidoff, a Latvian. In 1897, the family moved to London and settled in the East End. Although the Rosenbergs were poor, they had a particularly close family—eight children in all.

Rosenberg's formal education ended when he was 14, but he was from childhood an avid reader, and his later letters show an acquaintance with a surprising variety of English and American authors. After a brief apprenticeship at a firm of engravers in Fleet Street, Rosenberg was sponsored by three wealthy Jewish ladies and was able to attend the Slade School of Fine Art. He studied there from October 1911 to March 1914, winning several prizes for his paintings and even exhibiting some at the Whitechapel Gallery.

With the encouragement of his eldest sister, Rosenberg began writing poetry, and in 1912, he published at his own expense a small pamphlet of poems, *Night and Day*. It would be the first of three small, privately printed collections.

When the war broke out, Rosenberg was in South Africa visiting his sister; he had gone there hoping for an improvement in his health. In 1915 Rosenberg returned to England, and in May enlisted with the Suffolk Bantam Regiment. His remarks in a letter to his literary patron Edward Marsh reveal that his motive for joining was resignation rather than patriotic enthusiasm: "I never joined the army from patriotic reasons. Nothing can justify war. I suppose we must fight to get the trouble over."

He was transferred in early 1916 to the King's Own Royal Lancasters and sent to France the following June. He never rose above the rank of private, and for physical and temperamental reasons he found army life more difficult than most. Since he was Jewish, he may also have suffered from discrimination. His hatred for the war machine comes through in his letters. "Believe me," he wrote, "the army is the most detestable invention on earth, and nobody but a private knows what it is to be a slave."

Rosenberg spent nearly 20 months in the trenches or in areas near the trenches, with only two brief periods of rest. Given the material limitations of life in the trenches, Rosenberg increasingly turned away from painting, devoting himself entirely to his poetry.

Rosenberg was distinguished from the other war poets, first, by his Jewish origins, and then by his urban and working-class background, which meant he had no English pastoral nostalgia to set against front-line experience. The fact that he went through the war as a private also meant he saw that experience from a different perspective than the junior officer. But above all, Rosenberg is distinguished by the nature of his poetic talent. Most of his contemporaries had been formed in the Georgian mould, and had to adapt their basically conventional verse forms to sustain the weight of new experience; one sees this process very clearly in Sassoon. But Rosenberg, unburdened by this tradition, was from the beginning far more willing to experiment with poetic language. Unlike other poets whose poetic offerings is often seen as beginning and ending with the war, Rosenberg's poems of the war were a natural extension of the art he was making before he entered the trenches.

Rosenberg's connection to literary circles in London was tenuous at best. His friend from art school, Mark Gertler, introduced him to Edward Marsh, the classical scholar and career civil servant with private means whose five anthologies of *Georgian Poetry* sold thousands of copies and introduced poets like Owen and Brooke to the British public. Although Marsh read and critiqued Rosenberg's poems, encouraging him to continue writing and painting, the letters between the two men suggest that Marsh did not fully appreciate Rosenberg's poetry, which he found obscure and difficult. Rosenberg, in fact, is only represented once in the Georgian anthologies by a short extract from his verse play *Moses* in the 1916–17 volume. According to John Johnston, Rosenberg alienated a generation of postwar critics, who could find in his "Trench Poems" neither the aggressive social purpose of Sassoon nor the explicit spiritual appeal of Owen.

Rosenberg was killed in action during the Somme retreat on April 1, 1918. To this day, Rosenberg is perhaps the least known of the major war poets, although work of scholars such as Jon Silkin and Joseph Cohen have done much to make a convincing case for his inclusion in the English literary canon. ❋

Thematic Analysis of
"The Dead Heroes"

This 1914 poem, first published in *South African Women in Council,* concerns the sacrifice expected of England's young men. "The Dead Heroes" is an important reminder of the fullness of Rosenberg's account of the war; unlike Sassoon, who concentrated on the bitter betrayal of the soldiers by those at home, or Brooke, who only concerned himself with the nobility of self-sacrifice for one's country, Rosenberg's poems show him grappling with both the sublime and the horrendous in war. In part, this duality seems to stem from Rosenberg's own sense of dissatisfaction with the pre-war social order. Thus, while abhorring the war, he was yet unable to conceive of living the ordinary life of a civilian.

Critics have repeatedly been struck by the range and depth of Rosenberg's work. In part, this stems from his conscious use of poetry as a way of understanding and coping with the war. As he wrote in 1916, "I am determined that this war, with all its powers for devastation, shall not master my poeting; that is, if I am lucky enough to come through all right." He tried to understand all that the war stood for, meaning that he probably tried to expose the whole of himself to it. In one letter he describes this intention, "I will not leave a corner of my consciousness covered up, but saturate myself with the strange and extraordinary new conditions of this life." According to literary critic D. W. Harding, this willingness to open himself up to a new experience, rather than subdue the experience with his already established personality is "a large part, if not the whole secret of the robustness which characterizes his best work."

Rosenberg, as Harding notes, used this word "robustness" for something he felt to be essential to great poetry. In his fragment on Emerson, for instance, he writes, "The great poets of the earth have been mainly intellects with a kind of coarseness engrained. At the most delicate and rare there is a sense of solidity and bulk, close knit, that is like some unthinkably powerful chemical contained in some dewlike drop. We question a poet like Shelley because we feel this lack of robustness where we do not question Keats or Donne or Blake." Rosenberg's work possesses this same quality of robust reality.

In "The Dead Heroes," we get a glimpse at Rosenberg's early patriotism. While it lacks the self-referential and personal quality of Brooke's war sonnets, it is similarly enthusiastic. But if the sentiments expressed here are common enough to early war poetry, the imagery and language Rosenberg uses to convey these sentiments suggests an imaginative mind that was, as one critic noted with approval, "outracing the conventionalities of its subject and its theme." Reflecting the influence of William Blake's artistic vision, Rosenberg here explores a visionary world of "glorious skies," "mailed seraphim," "burning spears," and stars. Throughout the poem, Rosenberg invokes the flaming, ethereal world beyond the realm of human beings. This world, ready to welcome the new heroes, is brighter and more resplendent than the world the soldiers must leave behind.

The poem begins with an appeal to the skies to welcome those soldiers who had fallen in battle. Although they must relinquish their hold on life, the narrator promises them a new existence, "New days to outflame their dim / Heroic years." Their ascent to the afterlife unfolds in a triumphant crescendo of images: "Thrills their baptismal tread / The bright proud air; / The embattled plumes outspread / Burn upwards there / Flame out, flame out, O Song!"

In the final two stanzas of "The Dead Heroes," the soldiers are presented as being in a symbiotic relationship with England, which is at once the parent of the soldiers, "our children," and the product of the soldiers' sacrifice. As Rosenberg writes, "Their blood is England's heart; / By their dead hands / It is their noble part / That England stance." As we've seen in other war poems, the ultimate reward of heroic sacrifice is immortality, here presented as "Eternity" and "God's kiss," both for oneself and for one's country.

"The Dead Heroes" was written before Rosenberg had participated in the war himself. His later poems would reflect the harsher and more realistic view of war he gained after enlisting. By then, Rosenberg was no longer interested in poems that merely expressed patriotic emotions; in particular, he complained about Rupert Brooke's "begloried sonnets." The war, he continued, "should be approached in a colder way, more abstract, with less of the million feelings everybody feels; or all these should be concentrated in one distinguished emotion. Walt Whitman in 'Beat, drums, beat,' has said the noblest thing on war." ❀

Critical Views on
"The Dead Heroes"

[Bernard Bergonzi is the author of *Heroes' Twilight: A Study of the Literature of the Great War* (1965). In this selection from the book, Bergonzi identifies those qualities that distinguished Rosenberg from the other war poets, namely his Jewish and working-class origins and his exploratory method of using language.]

Rosenberg was distinguished from the other war poets, first, by his Jewish origins, and then by his urban and working-class background, which meant that he had no English pastoral nostalgia to set against front-line experience. And since he went through the war as a private he saw that experience in a different perspective from the junior officer. But above all, Rosenberg is distinguished by the nature of his poetic talent. Most of his contemporaries had been formed in the Georgian mould, and had to adapt their basically conventional verse forms to sustain a weight of new experience: one sees the process very clearly in Sassoon; but Rosenberg was from the beginning an experimenter, or perhaps an explorer, in his use of poetic language. His pre-war poems are numerous enough to show his originality of approach, and even if the war had not intervened there is every reason to suppose that the he would have continued his explorations. Unlike some of his slightly younger contemporaries, Rosenberg was not made into a poet by the war, but it both brought his gifts to a sudden maturity and cut them short. ⟨. . .⟩

One central aspect of Rosenberg's exploratory habit of language has been more precisely defined by D. W. Harding, in a valuable essay on Rosenberg:

> Rosenberg allowed his words to emerge from the pressure of a very wide context of feeling and only a very general direction of thought. The result is that he seems to leave every idea partly embedded in the undifferentiated mass of related ideas from which it has emerged.

One might, perhaps, gloss this by saying that rather often Rosenberg wasn't at all sure what he wanted to say when he was writing a poem:

the comparison of a sculptor plastically working on his statue and letting the conception grow accordingly isn't altogether exact, since clay and words are, of course, very different media. Certainly, one is much more aware of *process*, of composition as something continuous rather than a single act, in reading Rosenberg's poetry than with any of his contemporaries. But taking a less favourable view that Professor Harding's, I would be inclined to say that a great deal—perhaps most—of Rosenberg's earlier work is marred by a quality that could be called groping as much as exploration. A lot of this work seems to me incoherent and often desperately obscure. But this is no more than to say that it was the apprentice work of a dedicated and potentially powerful talent. ⟨. . .⟩

D. W. Harding has referred to the way in which Rosenberg fuses two apparently disparate attitudes, which as he puts it, 'express a stage of consciousness appearing before either simple attitude has become differentiated'. Certainly Rosenberg's imagination seems to have functioned dialectically, and this may have been both cause and effect of this great attachment to the poetry of Donne, of whom he wrote before the war, 'I have certainly never come across anything so choke-full of profound meaningful ideas. It would have been very difficult for him to express something commonplace if he had to.' The dialectical habit of mind, and the specific influence of Donne, are very apparent in one of Rosenberg's best, and best-known, poems, 'Break of Day in the Trenches', in which the dialectical movement is objectified by the figure of the rat, moving freely between the British and German trenches. The basic structure of the poem recalls Donne's 'The Flea'. The soldier in the trench is juxtaposed between two modest natural objects:

> The darkness crumbles away—
> It is the same old druid Time as ever.
> Only a live thing leaps my hand—
> A queer sardonic rat—
> As I pull the parapet's poppy
> To stick behind my ear.

Yet he does not employ them primarily for solace, as a means of escape from the destructive presence of war in the manner of, say, Blunden. The rat's function is to emphasize by his very freedom the arbitrary separation between the two front lines, and by his low, ugly vitality to point up the fact of human death:

It seems you inwardly grin as you pass
Strong eyes, fine limbs, haughty athletes
Less chanced than you for life. . . .

—Bernard Bergonzi, *Heroes' Twilight: A Study of the Literature of the Great War* (London: Constable, 1965): pp. 110–11, 115.

Horace Gregory on Rosenberg's Isolation

[Poet and critic Horace Gregory (1898–1982) taught poetry and advanced writing at Lawrence College in Bronxville, New York. He was also the author of *Pilgrim of the Apocalypse: A Critical Study of D. H. Lawrence* (1933), *Amy Lowell: Portrait of the Poet in Her Time* (1958), *The World of James McNeill Whistler* (1959), *The Dying Gladiators, and Other Essays* (1961), *Dorothy Richardson: An Adventure in Self-Discovery* (1967), and *The House of Jefferson Street: A Cycle of Memories* (1971). He received the Bollingen Prize for his *Collected Poems* in 1965. In this essay, which initially appeared in a 1946 issue of *Poetry*, Gregory considers the ways in which Rosenberg's isolation from the literary mainstream enabled him to meet his own standards of poetic responsibility.]

At the time of this resolution to write new poems came the War and his enlistment in the British Army. Among his ambitions was to write a play in verse, an ambition common to many "modern" poets in England, Ireland and the United States since Ellen Terry met with such success in a production of Tennyson's *Becket*. But whatever gifts Rosenberg possessed, they were not of the theatre, nor could he relate his themes of Hebraic origin to the disciplines of writing dramatic verse. Figures of Moses, of Saul, of Lilith, and at last, a vaguely conceived and heretical Unicorn in scenes with Nubians and Amazons crowded the pages he sent to Gordon Bottomley to read. What he accomplished here was not the first draft toward writing a play, but flexibility and a fresh approach to the writing of blank verse. He had rejected smoothness in writing verse; "Regular rhythms I do not like much" he wrote to Edward Marsh, and he made the choice of seeming obscure and being "experimental." It was his purpose to write out of and within the Jewish tradition, which in itself, aside from Milton's contribution to an almost Hebraic literature in *Paradise Lost*, was an "experimental" task in English verse; ⟨. . .⟩.

Since his death a few of Rosenberg's shorter poems have been reprinted in various anthologies which bring him back to mind as a "war poet," a survivor of the same moment and of like associations that surround the memory of Wilfred Owen; and of the two poets, Owen has remained in the more fortunate position. In latter-day revivals of Owen's name, the author of "I, too, saw God through mud—" has perhaps suffered the curse of being overrated, for like Rosenberg, his writings were cut short by death in military action in 1918. Owen was less radical, but also less fragmentary in his accomplishment than Rosenberg; in reading Owen, the reward is one of finding four or five completed poems that seem to exist for themselves alone; in reading Rosenberg, one finds the occasional line or the intractable phrase, or the presence of an isolated imagination that has evidence of life beyond the accomplishments of art. One has confidence that the coarser fibers of Rosenberg's poems were the necessary complements of what he had to say in poems that showed his hatred of war as well as the religious center of his being. His *August, 1914* is characteristic of the "war poems" that he had begun to write:

> What in our lives is burnt
> In the fire of this?
> The heart's dear granary?
> The much we shall miss?
>
> Three lives hath one life—
> Iron, honey, gold.
>
> The gold, the honey gone—
> Left is the hard and cold.
>
> Iron are our lives
> Molten right through our youth.
> A burnt space through ripe fields
> A fair mouth's broken tooth.

There is little self-pity in these lines, and unlike Owen, Rosenberg with his hopes of accomplishment fixed upon the "grave" and "austere" had no concern for

> the pity of war.

The Poetry is in the pity.

Rosenberg held to a darker faith:

Moses, from whose loins I sprung,
Lit by a lamp in his blood
Ten immutable rules, a moon
For mutable lampless men.

His darkness, whether in sight of trench warfare or in London's streets, was lighted only by such fragmentary lines as these:

Our eyes no longer sail the tidal streets,
Nor harbor where the hours like petals float
By sensual treasures glittering through thin walls
Of women's eyes and colour's mystery.
. . . .
God gives to glisten in an angel's hair
These he has gardened, for they please his eyes.

The imperfections in these lines are obvious enough; the repetitions of "eyes" within them are not placed with the necessary skill to build the lines into a finished poem. The merits are in the phrases, "tidal streets," the "thin walls of women's eyes," and the simple use of "gardened."

If Rosenberg did not accomplish much of what his poetry and prose implied, he leaves behind him a standard of intention and of poetic responsibility that has yet to be met by younger poets of the second World War. It is clear that like Owen he had broken with popular standards that had been accepted for poetry written before 1914. His example to younger poets of more than a generation later lies not in his failures, but in his concern for values in poetry that dismissed immediate influences, and sought out with appropriate seriousness the central forces, which in his life were religious, of poetic imagination and character.

——Horace Gregory, "The Isolation of Isaac Rosenberg," *Poetry: A Magazine of Verse* 68 (April–September 1946): pp. 35, 37–39.

DAVID DAICHES ON ROSENBERG'S PLACE IN ENGLISH
POETRY

[In this 1950 review of *The Collected Poems of Isaac Rosenberg*,
Daiches traces the development of Rosenberg's writing,
observing that the young poet seemed to be moving in an
entirely new and unique direction, uninfluenced by the literary endeavors of his contemporaries.]

At the time of his death Rosenberg was only beginning to find himself as a poet, and thus what we have of his work is in more than one
sense fragmentary. His early poems have a rich, almost lush, vocabulary and a startling sensuous violence: his problem was to learn to
control his images and subtilize his rhythms without losing his characteristic strength and liveliness. It is interesting to trace the development of this control, to note the gradual shedding of images
suggesting the overgrown romanticism of a poet like Beddoes in
favor of a more astringent verse. Yet he never seems to have come
under the influence of Hulme or Pound or the other preachers of a
spare, sinewy verse who were active in London just before and at the
beginning of the First World War. He was not moving towards anything reminiscent of "Prufrock" or even the controlled ironies of
Wilfred Owen's war poetry. He had begun as a painter (under the
kind and sometimes exasperating patronage of three Jewish ladies
who provided for his training at the Slade School) and this perhaps
accounts for his fiercely colorful imagery, so different from the pallid
precision of the Imagists. If he had lived he would not have become
just another poet in the Eliot group, but would have developed into
a poet much more like some members of the Apocalypse group who
emerged in England immediately before the Second World War. One
can almost see in him something of Dylan Thomas.

The parallel with Thomas (inaccurate, of course, as all such parallels are bound to be) can be drawn not only on the basis of the violence and richness in the verse of both poets, but also with respect to
their use of national and religious background. Thomas uses Welsh
folklore and Christian symbols together and distills a strange magic
by peppering both with Freud and surrounding the whole with a
profound personal emotion. Rosenberg did something similar with
his Jewish background. He drew on this background readily; he is in
fact one of the few English Jewish poets whose poetry quite unmis-

takably owes much of its quality to Biblical and other Hebrew sources; but he uses this material in an original, mythopeic manner, casting his own ironies and modernities around it until it develops an atmosphere quite different from anything to be found in Hebrew literature. ⟨. . .⟩

⟨. . .⟩ Had Rosenberg lived to develop further along the lines on which he had already moved, he might have changed the course of modern English poetry, producing side by side with the poetry of Eliot and his school a richer and more monumental kind of verse, opposing a new romantic poetry to the new metaphysical brand. But it is futile to speculate on the might-have-beens of history. Here are the poems, remarkable enough though incomplete, and, even as they are, a significant contribution to English poetry.

—David Daiches, "Isaac Rosenberg: Poet," *Commentary* 10 (July–December 1950): pp. 91–92, 93.

Thematic Analysis of
"Break of Day in the Trenches"

A version of "Break of Day in the Trenches" was most probably completed by the end of July 1916. It first appeared in the December 1916 issue of the Chicago journal *Poetry*. In an August 6 letter to Edward Marsh, Rosenberg described it as "a poem I wrote in the trenches, which is surely as simple as ordinary talk." It remains to this day one of Rosenberg's best-known poems.

"Break of Day in the Trenches" begins quietly. On the one hand, the reader feels a sense of uncertainty and anxiety about what the coming of dawn will bring; on the other hand, the speaker's familiarity with it—"the same old druid Time as ever"—suggests the soldier's weary resignation to the brutalities and dangers he knows the day will bring. The scene is then brought into focus by the startled movement of a rat, a "live thing." In "Break of Day in the Trenches" Rosenberg juxtaposes the soldier to natural objects, highlighting both the similarities and differences between them.

After the appearance of the rat, the soldier pulls a poppy out of the trench earth and puts it behind his ear. Rosenberg compares the soldier with poppies, an emblem of the British war dead, following the popularity of John McCrae's "In Flanders Fields." ("If ye break faith with us who die / We shall not sleep, though poppies grow / In Flanders field.") Poppies were thought to feed off the blood that had soaked into the earth, which turned their petals red. A short-lived flower, the poppy's transience mirrors that of the soldier's; even the careless moment when the soldier nonchalantly sticks a poppy behind his ear suggests how vulnerable the soldier, like the poppy, is. The poppy's connection with the dead will again be alluded to in the striking image at the end of the poem—"Poppies whose roots are in man's veins."

In the next lines, the rat underscores the arbitrary separation between the two front lines by his ability to travel freely back and forth between them. The rat calls to mind the imagery used by John Donne in his poem "The Flea," which plays on a similar idea, only in his case, for the purposes of courtship. (Rosenberg, like many of the First World War poets was heavily influenced by Metaphysical poets). Critics have also noted how the rat captures what some have called Rosenberg's "dialectical habit of mind." Characterized by the soldier as "droll" and "sardonic," the rat is seen as rising above both the ideological barriers and the physical obstacles of human beings. His willingness to alight in the hand of either a German or English soldier reveals his "cosmopolitan sympathies," which stand starkly at odds with the virulent nationalism that has imprisoned the soldiers within the narrow confines of their trenches. There is something ironic, too, in the idea that the two enemies—German and English—will be temporarily linked by their common acceptance of this measly rat. Rosenberg also uses the rat as a foil to the soldiers— its base vitality has more of a chance of survival than do the trained and physically fit soldiers—"Strong eyes, fine limbs, haughty athletes"—proudly amassed to do battle for their countries. The speaker then tries to imagine what the war must seem like from the perspective of the rat: "What do you see in our eyes / At the shrieking iron and flame / Hurled through still heavens?" In this role, the rat can thus be seen as the objectification of the soldier's (or Rosenberg's) mood. Rosenberg uses this perspective to both heighten the reader's sense of distance from the subjective, emotional intensity of the battle and to underscore the objective horrific nature of warfare.

In the second half of the poem, Rosenberg concentrates on the tragic nature of human beings' mutilation of themselves and nature. The fields of France are thus described as "torn" as easily and thoughtlessly as one might tear a piece of paper. This image suggests at once the power of modern weapons and the vulnerability of humanity and nature.

From here on the poem becomes more violent, as the ironic distance afforded by the brief moment of safety gives way to the reality of the violence and danger of the upcoming battle. The moment of truce and diversion offered by the appearance of the rat is over, and with it, the reprieve the soldier had gained from his own imminent death.

In the final lines of "Break of Day in the Trenches," Rosenberg returns to the poppy, the flower of the dead. He adds to this image the pregnant word "dust," which could refer either to the dust that whitens the poppy or the dust that covers the dead and to which all human beings must ultimately turn. ❦

Critical Views on
"Break of Day in the Trenches"

[In this forward to the 1937 edition of *The Collected Works
of Isaac Rosenberg*, Sassoon discusses the fusion between
English and Jewish culture that he sees occurring in Rosenberg's poetry.]

⟨. . .⟩ In reading and re-reading these poems I have been strongly
impressed by their depth and integrity. I have found a sensitive and
vigorous mind energetically interested in experimenting with language, and I have recognised in Rosenberg a fruitful fusion between
English and Hebrew culture. Behind all his poetry there is a racial
quality—biblical and prophetic. Scriptural and sculptural are the
epithets I would apply to him. His experiments were a strenuous
effort for impassioned expression; his imagination had a sinewy and
muscular aliveness; often he saw things in terms of sculpture, but he
did not carve or chisel; he *modelled* words with fierce energy and
aspiration, finding ecstasy in form, dreaming in grandeurs of superb
light and deep shadow; his poetic visions are mostly in sombre
colours and looming sculptural masses, molten and amply wrought.
Watching him working with words, I find him a poet of movement;
words which express movement are often used by him and are essential to his natural utterance.

Rosenberg was not consciously a 'war poet'. But the war destroyed
him, and his few but impressive 'Trench Poems' are a central point in
this book. They have the controlled directness of a man finding his
true voice and achieving mastery of his material; words and images
obey him, instead of leading him into over-elaboration. They are all of
them fine poems, but 'Break of Day in the Trenches' has for me a
poignant and nostalgic quality which eliminates critical analysis. Sensuous front-line existence is there, hateful and repellent, unforgettable
and inescapable. And beyond this poem I see the poems he might have
written after the war, and the life he might have lived when life began
again beyond and behind those trenches which were the limbo of all
sane humanity and world-improving imagination. For the spirit of
poetry looks beyond life's trench-lines. And Isaac Rosenberg was natu-

rally empowered with something of the divine spirit which touches
our human clay to sublimity of expression.

—Siegfried Sassoon, Forward to *The Collected Works of Isaac Rosenberg: Poetry, Prose, Letters, and Some Drawings,* ed. Gordon Bottomley
and Denys Harding (London: Chatto and Windus, 1937): pp. ix–x.

D. W. Harding on the Dialectical Imagination

[Although known mainly as literary critic, D. W. Harding
(1906–1993) was a psychologist by profession and served as
editor of *The British Journal of Psychology* as well as teaching
psychology at Bedford College in London for over two
decades. He is the author and editor of numerous works,
including *Isaac Rosenberg, The Collected Works of Isaac Rosenberg* (1937) (editor with Gordon Bottomley), *The Impulse to
Dominate* (1941), and *Rosenberg, Collected Poems* (1949)
(editor with Bottomley). In this essay from *Experience into
Words* (1963), Harding examines how Rosenberg's dissatisfaction with pre-war life and his complex feelings about the war
itself were translated into his work.]

His dissatisfaction with pre-war life had already shown itself in his
work, notably in the revolt against God which appears in several pas-
sages, God being taken as someone responsible for the condition of
the world and its established order:

Ah, this miasma of a rotting God!

And of the rotting God and his priests he exclaims:

Who has made of the forest a park?
Who has changed the wolf to a dog?
And put the horse in harness?
And man's mind in a groove?

In 'Moses', from which this passage comes, he was engrossed with the
theme of revolt against a corrupting routine; he presents Moses at
the moment of breaking free from the comfort of the usual and
politic by killing the overseer. Rosenberg never fully defined his atti-

tude to violence as distinct from strength, though there is a hint in his letters that 'The Unicorn' might have approached this question. In 'Moses' he accepts violence because it seems a necessary aspect of any effort to bring back the power and vigour of purpose which he felt the lack of in civilized life:

> I have a trouble in my mind for largeness.

It was because of this attitude to the pre-war world that Rosenberg, hating the war, was yet unable to set against it the possibilities of ordinary civilian life, and regret them in the way, for instance, that Wilfred Owen could regret them in 'Strange Meeting'. When Rosenberg wanted to refer to an achieved culture—rather than merely human possibilities—against which to measure the work of war he had to go back to remote and idealized Jewish history, producing 'The Burning of the Temple' and 'The Destruction of Jerusalem by the Babylonian Hordes'. More usually he opposed both to the war and to the triviality of contemporary civilization only a belief in the possibilities of life and a hope derived from its more primitive aspects:

> Here are the springs, primeval elements,
> The roots' hid secrecy, old source of race,
> Unreasoned reason of the savage instinct.

The root is the most important of the symbols which recur throughout his work, and birth, creation, and growth are his common themes.

> —D. W. Harding, *Experience into Words* (New York: Horizon Press, 1964): pp. 92–93.

Jean Moorcroft Wilson on Rosenberg's Paintings

[Jean Moorcroft Wilson is a writer whose work includes *Isaac Rosenberg, Poet & Painter* (1975) and *Siegfried Sassoon: The Making of a War Poet, a Biography (1896–1918)* (1999). In this selection from her biography of Rosenberg, Wilson considers how Rosenberg's background as a painter influenced and aided his work as a poet, specifically encouraging him to create the powerful visual images and bold compositions that characterize much of his best poetry.]

⟨. . .⟩ Apart from the sheer practical difficulties of drawing and painting under such conditions, by the time Rosenberg joined the army in late 1915 he had begun to believe in himself 'more as a poet than a painter'. After nearly a year as a soldier he was convinced that he was 'more deep and true as a poet than a painter'. He planned to teach drawing at a school a few days a week when he returned to civilian life, but only because this would leave him, he hoped, 'plenty of leisure to write'.

Rosenberg was undoubtedly correct in his choice, for he shows far more originality as a poet than painter. Yet part of his originality as a poet stems from his experience as a painter and the two cannot be separated. For there is a strong visual element in his poetry which helps to make up his unique quality. Even if we did not know that Rosenberg had sketched the troop-ship and louse-hunting, it would be quite clear from his poems on these two subjects that he had looked at his material with the painter's as well as the poet's vision. Phrases such as 'Grotesque and queerly huddled / Contortionists' and 'Nudes—stark and glistening' compel the reader to visualise the scene in a way which makes it more vivid.

When we consider the poetry of this last period in the context of his whole output it is important to remember the conditions under which it was written. Rosenberg realised that ideally the poet should 'wait on ideas, (you cannot coax real ones to you) and let as it were a skin grow naturally round and through them'. Yet he is forced through circumstances 'when the ideas come hot' to 'seize them with the skin in tatters, raw, crude, in some parts beautiful in others monstrous'. He was convinced that going into the army had retarded his development as a poet:

> As to what you say about my being luckier than other victims [he wrote to Schiff] I can only say that one's individual situation is more real and important to oneself than the devastations of fates and empires especially when they do not vitally affect oneself. I can only give my personal and if you like selfish point of view that I feeling myself in the prime and vigour of my powers (whatever they may be) have no more free will than a tree; seeing with helpless clear eyes the utter destruction of the railways and avenues of approaches to outer communication cut off. Being by the nature of my upbringing, all my

energies having been directed to one channel of activity, crippled from other activities and made helpless even to live. It is true I have not been killed or crippled, been a loser in the stocks, or had to forswear my fatherland, but I have not quite gone free and have a right to say something.

It could equally well be argued that the war made Rosenberg as a poet. In the appalling conditions on the Western Front he rejects the last vestiges of Romanticism still evident in his poetry as late as mid-1915. The harshness and horror of his own and others' existence undoubtedly focuses his perception and gives his work an immediacy and edge it previously lacked. His keen eye for the grotesque and his detached, almost impersonal attitude now show to their full advantage. His subject matter at last lends itself to his somewhat chaotic method of composition, where image is hurled upon image, the rhythms are highly irregular and form is not of prime importance. All that is best in Rosenberg's work comes to fruition in these final poems. Looking back, his earlier work can be seen as a groping but consistent preparation for the trench poems. The earliest Romantic and Pre-Raphaelite imitations show awkwardnesses which suggest that Rosenberg finds the mode unsuited or inadequate to his needs. While the poems of the middle period, with their experiments in free verse and wider variety of subject matter, indicate a more conscious rejection of a smooth technique. He now finds this inappropriate to the harsh vision he is at last beginning to realise, but which is not fully expressed until the trench poems.

—Jean Moorcroft Wilson, Isaac Rosenberg, Poet and Painter (London: Cecil Woolf, 1975): pp. 209–11.

Matt Simpson on Reading "Break of Day"

[Matt Simpson is a poet and critic who lectures at the Liverpool Institute of Higher Education. His works include *Windows Project* (1977), *Making Arrangements* (1982), *See You on the Christmas Tree* (1984), and *An Elegy for the Galosherman: New and Selected Poems* (1990). In this excerpt from an article entitled, "Only a Living Thing— Some Notes Towards a Reading of Isaac Rosenberg's 'Break of Day in the Trenches,'" Simpson offers a close reading of the opening lines of Rosenberg's well-known poem, focusing particularly on the ironic element introduced by the figure of the rat.]

A queer sardonic rat—

Here we have the third reckless dash of the poem; and the line re-establishes the three-stress rhythm of the first line and picks up, in the manner of internal rhyme, the 'a' sound . . . 'darkness'/ 'sardonic'. If we were directing a film crew here we would order our camera to move in rapidly from the wide-angled shot of a sky seen from a trench to a very near close-up, to zoom in on the rat's face as if searching it for an expression. We now have the famed pathetic fallacy: the poet discovers a chance companion and, wishing to grab hold of the moment in which something may be shared, projects his own mood, or aspects of it, on to the rat (compare Owen's encounter with the visionary 'enemy' in 'Strange Meeting'); a curious and moving tension of ironies—the otherness ('queer') of the rat and a familiarity ('sardonic', the poet recognising and humorously objectifying his own mood)—is at work again.

As I pull the parapet's poppy
To stick behind my ear.

We are back with the three-beat stress but this time the rhythm is spiced with an alliterative jauntiness, as if the plucking of the poppy is also a reflex action (again I find myself disagreeing with Holbrook who says 'here the alliteration emphasises the intentionality of the act'). At best it is half-conscious—but a more important point and one not to be missed is that the action is a killing one: the poppy will die as the result of such casualness. Notwithstanding, the devil-may-care attitude suggests something celebratory too: the making of a new friend—so that the poppy is worn like a token or garland to celebrate the fact that the poet and the rat (and the poppy—just about!) are alive, alive-o. It is also impossible to think of this gesture without also remembering the squaddie's Woodbine stuck behind the ear.

Droll rat, they would shoot you if they knew

. . . 'queer', 'sardonic', 'droll' . . . the rat is endowed with ironic humour: an item in its survival kit. And yet this humour is counterbalanced by a poignant sense of fragility represented in the plucked poppy, already implicitly an emblem of sacrifice. As with the 'vision' in Owen's 'Strange Meeting', the rat has become Rosenberg's doppel-gänger. And we cannot help relishing a further irony in the poet's actually entering into conversation with it in a situation patently and potently absurd. So *this* is the great experience of war: this *reductio ad absurdum,* a man talking to a rat in a trench at dawn! a dawn we may want, in imagination, to associate with executions! The collo-quial rhythm of this line rolls along on a pattern of ū sounds: 'shoot', 'you', and 'knew' echoing; and is stitched together by the two 'they's'—who, as far as I am concerned (though Lucas sees them as an indication of Rosenberg's Jewishness, the 'they's' becoming in his mind 'gentiles who think the world made for them and their especial virtues') represent something humorously, dangerously, conspirato-rially unspoken—absurdly vague someone-elses, the you-know-who-I-mean brass hats and politicians responsible for all this. Having the freedom to cross over into 'enemy' territory, the rat can claim cosmopolitan (richer in connotation than merely *national* or even *allied*) sympathies; poet and rat share the excitements of an intimate secret, something which 'they' luckily do not know about: dangerous knowledge, risky for both rat (the poet certain that it can be shot for it, as traitors or deserters are shot) and poet (involved in a complicity—his poem too having cosmopolitan sympathies able too, in imagination, to cross the sleeping green!). In this perilous instant, rat, poet and poem take their lives into their own hands: this instant when the wakeful poet/soldier dissociates himself (by virtue of his sympathies) from the company of haughty athletes, of either side, and soliloquises, in the manner of Hamlet talking to Yorick's skull, in front of a scampering unidealistic rat—the only being around in the breaking dawn alive and sympathetic enough to 'share' his tremulous humanity. The irony of this could hardly be more heartrending.

> Your cosmopolitan sympathies
> (And God knows what antipathies).

—Matt Simpson, "Only a Living Thing—Some Notes Towards a Reading of Isaac Rosenberg's 'Break of Day in the Trenches,'" *Critical Survey* 2, no. 2 (1990): pp. 131–32.

Thematic Analysis of
"Dead Man's Dump"

For many critics, "Dead Man's Dump" is Rosenberg's finest war poem and one of the most compete crystallizations of the war experience. Rosenberg described the origins of this poem in a letter to Edward Marsh, dated May 8, 1917: "Ive written some lines suggested by going out wiring, or rather carrying wire up the line on limbers and running over dead bodies lying about. I don't think that I've written is very good but I think the substance is, and when I work on it Ill make it fine. . . ." In this long poem, Rosenberg presents a number of different perspectives on the experience of combat. He culminates in a single snapshot of war's devastating blow to the mind and body.

The first three stanzas throw the reader directly into the sights and sounds of war. Rosenberg himself is an active agent in the moment, closely observing the grisly sight before him, hearing the bones crunch. In the first stanza, for instance, Rosenberg records soldiers' reaction to the supposed brutishness of the enemy, while their own barbarity goes unnoticed.

In the second stanza, Rosenberg records the visual and auditory images of running limbers (carriages used for ammunition and equipment) over dead bodies. The reader can't help but cringe, as Rosenberg implies the watcher does, when the bodies of dead soldiers are damaged. The bodies are described as if human; their mouths seem only temporarily shut, while they huddle together in purposeful action. The watcher himself identifies with the dead, drawn to them by their common humanity and by the shared experience of conflict. The shells cry out, just like the soldiers whose limbs are being torn apart by the exploding shells.

In the third stanza, there is a change in tone, as Rosenberg draws back to the perspective of Earth herself. The frenetic activities of the battlefield are measured against the ageless power of Earth, who is described as a jealous and hungry goddess. The death of the soldiers whose bodies are sprawled on the ground is now explained as part of a larger design. Earth "has waited for them, / All the time of their growth / Fretting for their decay: Now she has them at last!" This female image has desired the soldiers, and now she stops and fixes their youth when it is most beautiful. But unlike Keat's "Ode to a Grecian Urn" in which art fixes youthful lives in such a way that both the lives and the image interact to produce a sense of immortality, in Rosenberg's poem, death accomplishes this crystallization.

The fourth stanza is a series of questions, as the narrator demands to know the fate of the soldiers, even though he knows the answer. The one question left unanswered arrives at the end—"Who hurled them out? Who hurled?" Even if we know the answer to be humanity, we are still left to wonder why this was so.

Rosenberg asserts the human value of life. But unlike some of the other war poets, who might say that death alone makes life significant, Rosenberg in the next stanza considers what has been lost with Earth's suspension of these lives ("stopped and held"). In this and subsequent stanzas, Rosenberg laments both the "half used life" as well as the young men's oblivion to the danger, to the fact that they are living on borrowed time, until it is too late. "What of us who, flung on the shrieking pyre, / Walk, our usual thoughts untouched." Believing themselves to be immortal, it is only when "the flames beat loud on us" that a fear "may choke in our veins / And the startled blood may stop."

The next stanza reminds the reader of everything in the soldiers' environment that conspires against them. Even the shrapnel seems to take on an existence independent of the young men, deciding who among them will be killed and who will survive "in bleeding pangs."

In the ninth stanza, Rosenberg focuses on a particular death. The evidence of physical violence—"A man's brains splattered on / A stretcher-bearer's face"—are relayed matter-of-factly, but it is the soul's inaccessibility to human tenderness that becomes the focal point of the stanza.

Next Rosenberg himself seems to look up from the dead man before him to survey the landscape of dead bodies and contemplate the meaning of these bodies. There is something unnatural about the dead: they are "burnt black by strange decay" and seem sinister and silent. The dead are now identified by their loss of human identity; they are decomposing to become part of the earth, but even the earth, the grass and clay, seems more animate than those who are dead.

In the final stanzas of the poem, Rosenberg again makes the movement from general contemplation to the specific circumstance of an individual consciousness. A dying man reaches out his arms, imploring for aid or simply an end to the suffering. "Will they come? Will they come?" The failure to reach him in time becomes representative of the war's inevitable erosion. "Here is not one long dead; / His dark hearing caught our far wheels. . . ." The poem ends as it began, with the limber crushing the dead: "And our wheels grazed his dead face."

As Marius Bewley has noted, Rosenberg stands apart from other war poets in his awareness that the suffering of war is too great to be comforted, with the result that in his poetry, suffering achieves something like "classical composure." Writing about "Dead Man's Dump," Bewley adds,

> It is directly, even starkly, concerned with suffering, and yet its terrible picture of agony never hinders the poise, the freedom of inquiry that is maintained throughout. In this poem, so impersonal and detached in comparison with much of Owen's poetry, there is a hard, almost shocking, concreteness and immediacy of imagery that makes Owen seem vague and general by contrast. . . . One is not so much aware of the single, the private, death here, as one is aware of the representative and universal quality in the death which it described.

In his measured, unflinching gaze at human pain, Rosenberg is able to achieve one of the fullest understandings of human dignity. ✿

Critical Views on
"Dead Man's Dump"

[This excerpt comes from a 1914 lecture that Rosenberg
gave while in South Africa, which was then printed in the
periodical *South African Women in Council*. In the lecture,
Rosenberg expresses his thoughts on art as an interpretive
and unifying agent of reality.]

We all, more or less, feel a work of art, and I should like in this paper
to find a sort of philosophic connection between one's thoughts and
work created by mind.

I also want to say a word on modern aims; and no doubt all here
have heard of the fermented state of culture now in Europe. The
multiplexity, and elaborately interwoven texture of modern life; the
whole monstrous fabric of modernity is rapidly increasing in complexity, and art, which is a sort of summing up, and intensification
of the spirit of the age, increases its aims accordingly. A great genius
is, at once, the product and the creator of his age. It is in him that a
marked stage of evolution is fulfilled. His ideas are absorbed and
permeate, even when the natures who fell them are not large enough
to contain them. These ideas weaken as they become absorbed into
the indrawing and everwidening complexities of life, and no longer
have their original force, and a new stimulus is necessary. So we have
these new movements and their energetic repudiation of preceding
movements. To make my point clear I shall be obliged to run
roughly through the evolution of art, before I can speak of its present state.

We all have impressions from nature. Our consciousness of these
impressions is life. To express and give shape to such impressions on
our consciousness, by artificial means, is art. Man's natural necessi-
ties, his instinct to communicate his desires, and feelings, found
shape in corresponding signs and sounds; symbols which, at first
crude, gradually developed and refined. Special emotions found
expression in the nearest and most sufficient ways. Singing and
dancing for joy—for awe and worship, the reverential mien and
solemn incantation. Victories, festivities, marriage, love, all these

were occasions for art. Shouting became singing; more and more rhythmical and orderly. From the expression of private joy and sorrow, it told tales of others' joys and woes. It became art. Hunters whose eyes were keen and hands were skilful, gloating over the image of the power they chased, strove to record it, cutting sharply with their rude hunting knives on the stone of their rough cave dwelling. Architecture developed, then sculpture as a natural result. We begin with high culture at the Egyptians. A land of high profound, austere philosophy—their art expressed their priestly natures. Art went hand in hand with their religion, grave and austere. With a profound knowledge of form and perfect craftsmanship, all their energies were directed to express deity, an abstraction of simple, solemn profundity, the omnipresent spirit. Their art was angular and severe.

The Greeks followed, more idealistic they cultivated a more effeminate conception of beauty, an idea of grace, of rounded forms, suavity. Body's strength and body's beauty, was the ideal of this lovely land, and this pagan philosophy has produced art, beautiful indeed, but of no intensity, no real hold on man's spirit.

We are moved by a work of art. Is an artistic emotion similar to an ordinary emotion got from actual life? Is fear, horror, pride, called into play? Yet we are moved, aesthetically. What moves us? Just as figures stand for quantities, so we have subtle but intelligible symbols to correspond to the most delicate and imperceptible shade of emotion; and it is by bringing these varied symbols into a coherent unity that a work of art is constructed. To detach a part from nature, and give it the completeness of the whole, by applying to that part the principle of rhythmic law that is instinctive in our consciousness, and harmonises us to the exterior nature. A law of repetition and contrast, continuity in variety. It is this principle that our consciousness responds to. Art becomes by this, a living thing, another nature, a communicable creation. To convey to all, in living language, some floating instant in time, that mixing with the artist's thought and being, has become a durable essence, a separate entity, a portion of eternity. Art widens the scope of living by increasing the bounds of thought. New moods and hitherto unfelt particles of feeling are perpetually created by these new revelations, this interfusion of man's spirit, eager to beget, and crowd existence with every finer possibility. Thus art is an intensification and simplification of life, which is fragmentary, and has no order and no coherent relationship to us, until it has passed through the crucible of Art. Science explains nature physically by atoms; philosophy explains life morally, but art interprets and intensifies life, representing a portion through the laws of unity that govern the whole.

—Isaac Rosenberg, "Art" (Lecture, Summer 1914). In *The Collected Works of Isaac Rosenberg: Poetry, Prose, Letters, Paintings and Drawings,* ed. Ian Parsons (New York: Oxford University Press, 1979): pp. 289–91.

MARIUS BEWLEY ON ROSENBERG'S STRENGTHS COMPARED TO WILFRED OWEN

[Marius Bewley was Professor of English at Rutgers University and the author of such works as *The Complex Fate: Hawthorne, Henry James, and Some Other American Writers* (1952), *The Eccentric Design: Form in the Classic American Novel* (1959), *Masks and Mirrors: Essays in Criticism* (1970), and *The English Romantic Poets: An Anthology* (editor) (1970). He also served on the editorial board of *Hudson Review* and was a contributor to many publications, including *Spectator, New Statesman, Partisan Review,* and *Southern Review.* In this excerpt from his essay, "The Poetry of Isaac Rosenberg," Bewley compares the poetry of Rosenberg to that of Wilfred Owen.]

For every person who has read a poem of Rosenberg's, a few hundred must have read something of Wilfred Owen's. And yet Rosenberg is the greater poet. Both men were rather like unguilty angels who had fallen with the rout into pandemonium, and their verse is an attempt to survey creatively their new midnight universe. Owen may have carried a little more of the old heaven with him, but Rosenberg understood better the brutal anonymity of the war, and the true dimensions of the tragedy. Owen never quite became more than a good Georgian, and while it would be rash to speculate about the course of his literary career had he lived, his work has none of the rampant, impatient eagerness to reach beyond itself which is so frequently startling in the other poet's work. There was something Wordsworthian about the Georgians, but it was a Wordsworth stripped of stature; and it is stature that one never quite discovers in Owen's own poems. His hatred of war is too excessively a hatred of its physical effects on the lives of the young Englishmen under his command.

One cannot help feeling that Owen is caught and held back by the sight of all the suffering—which, after all, is only one anguished corner of the whole intolerable picture. Owen seems little concerned with any reality that is not to be penetrated by pity alone. He seems to converge his perspective lines toward the hospital cot rather than to unfold them from that terminus of pity. The vision he offers is poignant but incomplete, and too regretful to be great. It is a picture made up of many moving accidents—so many that the form of the tragedy is sometimes obscured.

Rosenberg's poetry does not stop short of the pity and tenderness in Owen's, but passes beyond it into something new. He is aware that the suffering of war is too great to be comforted, and he cannot mistake pity for succor; in his poetry, suffering achieves something like classical composure. Details are lost in bold simplicity of form, and his victims have a heroic moral strength, a stoicism which invites the mind not to the frustrating pity of helplessness, but to something like the re-creative pity of the ancient stage.

As an example of this attitude one may look at a short passage from "Dead Man's Dump," one of the greatest poems of World War I. It is directly, even starkly concerned with suffering, and yet its terrible picture of agony never hinders the poise, the freedom of inquiry that is maintained throughout. In this poem, so impersonal and detached in comparison with much of Owen's poetry, there is a hard, almost shocking, concreteness and immediacy of imagery that makes Owen seem vague and general by contrast:

> A man's brains splattered on
> A stretcher-bearer's face;
> His shook shoulders slipped their load,
> But when they bent to look again
> The drowning soul was sunk too deep for human tenderness.
> They left the dead with the older dead,
> Stretched at the cross roads.
> Burnt black with strange decay

Their sinister faces lie,
The lid over each eye,
The grass and coloured clay
More motion have than they
Joined to the great sunk silences.

One is not so much aware of the single, the private, death here, as one is aware of the representative and universal quality in the death which is described. All "the older dead" and all who will die seem to participate symbolically in this one soldier's death. The ineffectual resentment we might otherwise feel is guarded against by very carefully handled suggestions of inevitability, and, even as we watch, the action reaches and seems to continue beyond that point where human tenderness can follow, down into an antique, stoic, underworld of "great sunk silences." This soldier is less a private person than a point at which the fate of men in war becomes for a moment visible.

And it is significant that no facile, gratuitous commentary on that fate is offered in the whole eighty-six lines of "Dead Man's Dump." The poem's strength lies in the composure it maintains when faced by human pain, in its refusal to indulge an easy grief or extend an invitation to tears. It shows a sure control of words moving through dangerous emotions at disciplined speeds and leading the reader, by their very restraint and poise, into a fuller understanding of human dignity.

> —Marius Bewley, *Masks & Mirrors: Essays in Criticism* (New York: Athenum, 1970): pp. 288–90.

JEAN LIDDIARD ON THE HALF-USED LIFE

[Jean Liddiard is the author of *Isaac Rosenberg: The Half Used Life* (1975) and *Working for Victory: Images of Women in the First World War, 1914–1918* (1987). In this excerpt from her biography of Isaac Rosenberg, Liddiard discusses the roots of Rosenberg's more detached style (as compared to Owen's more emotional response) in light of his isolation from much of the pre-war pastoral English culture.]

Rosenberg's more detached approach becomes clearer if it is compared with that of other poets writing from the trenches. Wilfred Owen's "Anthem for Doomed Youth" is also a meditation on the fate of men in war, and like Rosenberg's poem it begins with a question: "What passing-bells for these who die as cattle?" Owen shows his emotional responses much more readily than Rosenberg, in the extreme emphasis of the doomed youth of the title (compared to the objectivity of "August 1914"), and the angry indignation of "cattle". Rosenberg reveals his only through the phrase "heart's dear granary"—the only explicit description of personal feeling in the poem. And in itself it is not simply a general expression of tenderness but conveys also a precise sense of rare or precious, that has been worked for and achieved. The tension of Owen's poem comes from the ironic opposition of the actual indignity of death in this war, and traditional ways of dignifying it:

> No mockeries now for them; no prayers nor bells,
> Not any voice of burning save the choirs,——
> The shrill, demented choirs of wailing shells;
> And bugles calling for them from sad shires.

The religion that created a civilization has not saved it. Owen has not only lost faith in it but feels betrayed by its failure; all vitality has been transferred to inhuman elements; it is the guns that show "monstrous anger", the shells that "shriek". Owen's indignation comes out in this sense of human feelings not merely annihilated but deformed, like the bodies of the men. The beautiful last line again evokes, in the "bugles" and "shires", a traditional order, and suggests at first the transcendent power, in spite of all, of human pity and grief. Its sweetness comes in fact from its nostalgia—not only that order of life, but that order of death has been finally destroyed.

There is no similar regret and consequent sense of personal outrage in Rosenberg's work, because he did not mourn that culture (both social and literary), summed up in Owen's "sad shires". In reply to Miss Seaton, who had it seems expressed a sense of loss similar to Owen's, Rosenberg remarked with his usual honesty from hospital on 15 November 1916 that the English countryside beloved of most post-Romantics did not mean much to him:

> London may not be the place for poetry to keep healthy in, but Shakespeare did most of his work there, and Donne, Keats, Milton, Blake—I think nearly all our big poets. But, after all, this is a matter of personal likings or otherwise. Most of the French country I have seen has been

devastated by war, torn up—even the woods look ghastly with their shell-shattered trees; our only recollections of warm and comfortable feelings are the rare times amongst human villages, which happened about twice in a year; but who can tell what one will like or do after the war? If the twentieth century is so awful, tell me what period you believe most enviable. Even Pater points out the Renaissance was not an outburst—it was no simultaneous marked impulse of minds living in a certain period of time—but scattered and isolated.

His sense of the past related to people he cared about, not to a pastoral memory or an "English way of life". Again he makes this clear in a poem called "Home thoughts from France", with its echoes of Browning's "Home Thoughts from Abroad", and its deliberate divergence from "O to be in England" sentiments.

> Wan, fragile faces of joy!
> Pitiful mouths that strive
> To light with smiles the place
> We dream we walk alive.
>
> To you I stretch my hands,
> Hands shut in pitiless trance
> In a land of ruin and woe,
> The desolate land of France.

The sadness here is not only nostalgia, but one more familiar to Rosenberg, a sense of being outcast. In the trenches, the experience of being cut off from the warmth of the familiar became usual for all the men there. The work of the other war poets, however different Sassoon, Owen, Thomas and Blunden were from each other, had one thing in common, a sense of emotional shock at this which comes out of anger, pity, or escape into the memory of happier times. This was not so with Rosenberg. Whatever else, he was not shocked by the war. He knew already about the "hard and cold".

—Jean Liddiard, *Isaac Rosenberg: The Half Used Life* (London: Victor Gollancz, 1975): pp. 204–6.

DESMOND GRAHAM ON ROSENBERG BETWEEN LIFE AND DEATH

[In this selection from Graham's book, *The Truth of War: Owen, Blunden, Rosenberg,* he discusses Rosenberg's fascination with the wounded who occupy a transitory space between life and death.]

⟨. . .⟩ Here, more directly than anywhere else, Rosenberg depicts the landscape of the trenches. We start with 'limbers', carts, with their freight of barbed wire, which in war's terms is part of a comprehensible desire for defence against a feared enemy and yet, as the carts pass the dead, the true absence of division within the battlefield is proved: friend and foe lie together, identical.

> The plunging limbers over the shattered track
> Racketed with their rusty freight,
> Stuck out like many crowns of thorns,
> And the rusty stakes like sceptres old
> To stay the flood of brutish men
> Upon our brothers dear.
>
> The wheels lurched over sprawled dead
> But pained them not, though their bones crunched,
> Their shut mouths made no moan,
> They lie there huddled, friend and foeman,
> Man born of man, and born of woman,
> And shells go crying over them
> From night till night and now.

'Earth has waited for them', natural and sinister in its practice of mortality. 'Now she has them at last!', not declined and old, but 'In the strength of their strength/Suspended—stopped and held.'

Rosenberg wonders what discoveries they must have made at the moment of death. Surely, so alive, and suffering so powerful a change, they must have been brought some new vision? But 'None saw their spirits' shadow shake the grass,'

> Or stood aside for the half used life to pass
> Out of those doomed nostrils and the doomed mouth
> When the swift iron burning bee
> Drained the wild honey of their youth.

He then considers the force of life in those who are still living. They walk, their 'usual thoughts untouched,' seemingly immortal because surviving. But they are full of the fear that they may be killed simply by terror, although their bodies are untouched by war. Those who are dead, 'Timelessly now, some minutes past', 'strode time with vigorous life', therefore the living are exactly as the dead were before 'the shrapnel called "an end!"' The gap between the living and the dead, so absolute, is incomprehensible.

So Rosenberg turns his tenderness, towards those between life and death, the wounded, seeking in them an understanding of the transition from the one state to the other. Some, 'in bleeding pangs', dream of home, 'Dear things, war-blotted from their hearts', as they are carried on stretchers. There is a possibility of return to the humane world. The war does not possess everyone till their end. This hope Rosenberg immediately counters. Even borne from the battlefield, one is not immune, one is still within the reach of death. Reached by death, one is beyond care, beyond the reach of the living ⟨. . .⟩.

⟨. . .⟩ All round the man who is dying, there is the world of the living, the world which Rosenberg himself inhabits. Rosenberg's implication in this world breaks off his contact, and he defines the distance between living and dead, the dying man and himself with the inevitability and disconnectedness of the word 'So', 'So we crashed round the bend. . .'.

Throughout his poems of war Rosenberg uses the first person plural pronouns 'we', 'our' and 'us', with a full sense of identification. He has no need to be spokesman for he writes, naturally, as one of the men: the community who look, in 'Returning, We Hear the Larks', to 'a little safe sleep'; who share the comic and violent release of hunting for lice. They are a brotherhood, united and strengthened by a consciousness that they are distinct from 'them': from those who would shoot the rat because it touched a German's hand; who would give 'all earth' to chaos because of their 'militant purpose'. They are a community, sharing the anguish of knowing that they have been divided unnaturally and completely from those who would give them a lover's tenderness or a smile of encouragement. They possess a common knowledge of their identity as the exploited, and this is their strength. It is a strength which is powerless to reach across death.

Rosenberg, in 'Dead Man's Dump', having focused the intensity of his curiosity upon the absolute gap between being vital and being dead, writes at the same time of the reality and the immediate impotence of the community of which both are part. As the dying man's feelings reach out with desperation towards his fellows, they are impelled towards him by the impersonal course of war. The living and the dying are of the same community, existing within touching distance and yet the touch, when it comes, is that of the wheels of a cart.

Those killed, though unreachable, are not separable from us. Their deaths do not leave us, for they are part of the world in which we would claim to live with responsibility and meaning. At the same time, for the soldier, there is the pain of helplessness. For us there is the awareness that men, capable of the most intense tenderness and compassion, are reduced through the very environment which arouses such feelings in us as we read, to brutal and impotent participation.

—Desmond Graham, *The Truth of War: Owen, Blunden, Rosenberg* (Manchester, England: Carcanet, 1984): pp. 154–55, 156–57.

JON SILKIN AND THE "IDEA" IN ROSENBERG

[In this selection from his book, *Out of Battle,* Silkin analyzes Rosenberg's desire to ensure that what he called the "idea" in his poetry would remain uncorrupted by technical conventions.]

⟨. . .⟩ Rosenberg belonged to no movement and apparently followed none of the critical dicta offered either by groups of poets or by individual critics. He had read some F. S. Flint and wrote to Miss Seaton in 1912:

> I suppose [his] poems give me pleasure because of their newness to me. . . . they seem to me just experiments in versification except some, which are more natural . . . those are the ones I like best. I like of the first lot, 'The heart's hunger', for the energy intensity and simplicity with which it expresses that strange longing for an indefinite ideal; the haunting desire for that which is beyond the reach of hands. I like the

one call[ed] 'Exultation', very much. The image in the last stanza; of the—

> '*birds, unrooted flowers of space,*
> Shaking to heaven a silver chime of bells',

I think is fine

What he identifies in Flint accords with what he elsewhere claims to admire in poetry: 'the energy intensity and simplicity' and, from his reading of Donne, the comprehensive, metaphysical handling of, and insight into, naturally occurring phenomena. Rosenberg's 'more natural' may seem at first to be overly reserved, but it remains a useful corrective. It points to his centrally poised achievement in which he is not symbolically, metaphysically, or realistically weighted in any one direction. His imagination nearly always illuminates observed phenomena, and is not an egocentric reworking of these as a metaphor for his thinking. However necessary we may still find the Imagist demands, their concentration on linguistic means, their fragmentation of the problem is implicitly commented on by Rosenberg's achievement. Only the best imagistic poems, such as Read's 'The Happy Warrior', and 'Hugh Selwyn Mauberley', are as *whole,* as entirely congruous, as the best of Rosenberg. Eliot's 'The Hollow Men', for instance, remains disappointingly thin.

Perhaps what Rosenberg most responded to in the Flint passage quoted above was the imaginative use of the strongly visual root image. There are few traces of Imagism in his work, although there are instances of a corresponding economy of expression—perhaps the clearest being 'August 1914':

Iron are our lives
Molten right through our youth.
A burnt space through ripe fields
A fair mouth's broken tooth.

These last two lines strike the imagist tone, partly I think because of their apparent impersonal handling of observed phenomena; but examination shows that these lines are in apposition to the previous two, that is, they extend an avowedly personal assertion.

What Rosenberg was working for was the 'idea', and it is something he repeatedly visualizes in his letters. As he wrote to Miss Seaton in 1916,

It is much my fault if I am not understood, I know; but I also feel a kind of injustice if my idea is not grasped and is *ignored* [my italics], and only petty cavilling at form, which I had known all along was so, is continually knocked into me.

To Bottomley, on 23 July of that year, he writes with extraordinary complexity and insight:

Simple *poetry,*—that is where an interesting complexity of thought is kept in tone and right value to the dominating idea so that it is understandable and still ungraspable. . . . I am always afraid of being empty.

This concern with 'idea' and its negative fear of emptiness are neither the concern of the Georgians nor the Imagists. For Rosenberg the idea was not only important, but was the controlling impulse driving the technical means. Denys Harding, one of his editors, believes that the operating idea began for Rosenberg at an early stage in the language-inducing process:

like so many poets in some degree, one supposes—[he] brought language to bear on the incipient thought at an earlier stage of its development. Instead of the emerging idea being racked slightly so as to fit a more familiar approximation of itself, and words found for *that,* Rosenberg let it manipulate words almost from the beginning, often without insisting on the controls of logic and intelligibility.

I suppose that for those who look askance at Rosenberg, Harding's last comment will seem appropriate, but what Harding is speaking of is the poet's process of making. It might be added that, by implication, much of that over-finished quality in English poetry before and since Rosenberg is criticized by his poetry, and perhaps, even, by Harding's commentary.

It seems as if Rosenberg's capacity as a painter, as a thinker in images, impelled him into regarding the 'idea' as the crucial component in the 'made thing', and that, although language was for him an apter medium than paint, the idea even so must never be 'racked' by something already familiar and existing *in language or diction;* but must select for itself the right, singular language incepting the image and tone, as close to the original but composed force as possible. The fumbling in his early work seems not that of a searching for a theme, but the attempt to find that language for his ideas which had not before him existed. It is his struggle (which becomes a present but never obtrusive part of the made thing)—a refusal to simplify a complex set of powerful active ideas—which makes his work rich and responsive. This is perhaps one sense of the 'root', which appears so persistently in his work, and which approximates a cluster of concerns gradually discovered, worked, and expressed, the 'flower' of which is the explicit, 'naturalistic' part of the poem. The idea which is 'understandable and still ungraspable' is inherent in the poem and cannot be abstracted from it, because its full and proper expression is its sensuous ramification—the poetry itself. The experience of the idea is the poem. To extract the idea would be to destroy it, because that would mean destroying its profound sensuous connections with the society that nourishes it. An idea is a social thing (and an individual one) organic to the society it grows in, and to the natural forces that society itself draws on for nourishment. That society is made aware of itself and those forces by the emerging idea. The individual particularizes the idea.

—Jon Silkin, *Out of Battle: The Poetry of the Great War,* 2nd ed. (London: Macmillan, 1998): pp. 258–60.

Thematic Analysis of
"A Worm Fed on the Heart of Corinth"

This brief poem written by Rosenberg in 1916 is best understood by taking into account Rosenberg's thoughts on the state of civilization both before the war and in light of subsequent developments in the fighting. In the poem, Rosenberg likens the fate of England with that of older, decadent, now deceased civilizations: Corinth, Babylon, and Rome.

The ancient city of Corinth, for instance, was involved in most of the political conflicts of Greece, but chiefly as a pawn in the struggles of more powerful city-states because of the strategic value of its citadel. In 44 B.C., Julius Caesar reestablished Corinth as a Roman colony. The new Corinth flourished and became the administrative capital of the Roman province of Achaea, but after the Turkish conquest in 1458, it was reduced to a country town. In a similar way, Babylon, one of the most famous cities of antiquity, was at one point declared by Herodotus to be the world's most splendid city. A center of literary and commercial activity, Babylon was also a target for foreign conquerors. And the decline and fall of the Roman Empire was, of course, a well-known subject by Rosenberg's time.

Rosenberg turns to another well-known story of political downfall, referring to Helen of Troy, said to be the most beautiful woman in Greece. As the story goes, Paris' seduction of her (she was the wife of Menelaus, king of Sparta) and refusal to return her was the cause of the Trojan War. To recover Helen, the Greeks launched a great expedition under the overall command of Menelaus' brother, Agamemnon, king of Argos or Mycenae. The Trojans refused to return Helen, and, assisted by allies from Asia Minor and Thrace, they managed to withstand a Greek siege for 10 years.

In Rosenberg's telling of the story, however, "Not Paris raped tall Helen, / But this incestuous worm, / Who lured her vivid beauty / To his amorphous sleep." The "worm" is Satan, here given the attributes of "shadowless," "amorphous," and "amorous." Then Rosenberg makes the connection to England unmistakable: like Helen, England is betrothed to Satan and thus seems destined for a historically inevitable downfall, like that of the other empires alluded to at the beginning of the poem. Yet Rosenberg's use of the word "betrothal" implies that England's marriage to Satan has not yet been consummated; thus, there is still time for moral redemption and escape.

Rosenberg's criticism of England's decadence reappears throughout his work. His social and artistic isolation, stemming from his Jewish and lower-class background, made him wary of many of the conventions—literary and social—of the day; he felt these conventions led to a kind of cultural atrophy. Rosenberg found release and escape in his own work, as a prose fragment on modern art reveals:

> The renaissance was the revival of learning. Civilization has been tamed by the commercial spirit, a logic without imagination, technical, scientific, practical. . . . Life stales and dulls, the mind demands noble excitement, half-apprehended surprises, delicate or harsh, the gleams that haunt the eternal desire, the beautiful. It is a vain belief that Art and life go hand in hand. Art is as it were another planet, which does indeed reflect the rays of life, but is, nevertheless, a distinct and separate planet!

Unlike Brooke, who felt himself one "whom England bore, shaped, made aware," Rosenberg had no allegiances to any abstract concept of England, only to individuals, to his family and friends. Some critics have argued that Rosenberg's un-romantic assessment of pre-war England enabled him to accept the war imaginatively as a totally embracing way of life, even while finding it morally and socially destructive. This, in turn, explains his more detached, even dispassionate language. ❁

Critical Views on
"A Worm Fed on the Heart of Corinth"

JOSEPH COHEN ON THE FALL OF EMPIRE

[Joseph Cohen is a former Professor of English at the University of Texas, Austin. His work includes a contribution to *The Poets and Their Critics, Volume III: Wilfred Owen* (James Reeves, editor); *Journey to the Trenches: The Life of Isaac Rosenberg* (1975) (editor and contributor); *Critical Essays on Dannie Abse* (editor) (1983); and *Bibliography of the Works of and Criticism About Dannie Abse* (editor) (1985). He is also a frequent contributor to Jewish newspapers and other literary journals. In this excerpt from his biography of Rosenberg, Cohen discusses how the sentiments expressed in "A Worm Fed on the Heart of Corinth" about the state of England became more fully developed in Rosenberg's prose work.]

Rosenberg spent the summer of 1917 in relative safety. He was still going up the line at night, but the routine was fixed, and so far nothing had happened. The possibility of death had not been minimized; he simply grew accustomed to it. He had become more a creature of the field than of the city. The oppressiveness and degradation of urban existence that he had known earlier, and his forebodings arising from it, were transformed into part of his literary landscape:

> *A worm fed on the heart of Corinth,*
> *Babylon and Rome:*
> *Not Paris rapes tall Helen,*
> *But this incestuous worm,*
> *Who lured her vivid beauty*
> *To his amorphous sleep.*
> *England! famous as Helen*
> *Is thy betrothal sung*
> *To him the shadowless,*
> *More amorous than Solomon.*

The war had made England vulnerable. She was betrothed to 'that incestuous worm' Satan, and Rosenberg prophesies her downfall if the marriage is consummated. In this fragment Rosenberg again fol-

lowed his technique of pulling together the disparate elements of a
motif developed earlier, reinforcing it with his new power, operating
mythopoeically. Of this poem Frank Kermode and John Hollander
have written: 'this prophecy of the fall of empire ranks perhaps
highest among Rosenberg's visionary fragments.'

But Rosenberg had much more to say on the subject, and in the
summer months he tried hard to gather his scattered thoughts and
feelings into a coherent artifact which would both signal and record
the end of a civilization. Death, he realized, had long stalked the
cities, and through the war, had spread to the countryside, devastating the normal intercourse of life, rooting out and eradicating the
sustaining force of human love.

> —Joseph Cohen, *Journey to the Trenches: The Life of Isaac Rosenberg
> 1890–1918* (London: Robson Books, 1975): pp. 164–65.

Paul Fussell on the Life of Isaac Rosenberg

[Paul Fussell gained critical acclaim—a National Book Critics
Circle Award and National Book Award in 1976—for his *The
Great War and Modern Memory*. Having served as Professor
of English at Rutgers University and the University of Penn-
sylvania, Fussell is also the author or editor of such works as
Ordeal of Alfred M. Hale, Leo Cooper (Editor) (1975), *Poetic
Meter and Poetic Form* (1979), *Abroad: British Literary Trav-
eling Between the Wars* (1980), *Siegfried Sassoon's Long
Journey: Selections from the Sherston Memoirs* (Editor) (1983),
and *The Norton Book of Travel* (Editor) (1987). In this excerpt
from *The Great War and Modern Memory*, Fussell discusses
Rosenberg's use of the pastoral tradition in images like the
poppy to conveying his experience of the war.]

⟨. . .⟩ So Rosenberg begins:

The darkness crumbles away—
It is the same old druid Time as ever,
Only a live thing leaps my hand—

"You might object to the second line as vague," he wrote Marsh, "but that was the best way I could express the sense of dawn." Despite the odd way the darkness dissipates in tiny pieces (like the edge of the trench crumbling away), the dawn is the same as in any time or place: gray, silent, mysterious. "Only" on this occasion there's something odd: as the speaker reaches up for the poppy, a rat touches his hand and scutters away. If in Frye's terms the sheep is a symbol belonging to the model—that is, pastoral or apocalyptic—world, the rat is the creature most appropriate to the demonic. But this rat surprises us by being less noisome than charming and well-traveled and sophisticated, perfectly aware of the irony in the transposition of human and animal roles that the trench scene has brought about. Normally men live longer than animals and wonder at their timorousness: why do rabbits tremble? why do mice hide? Here the roles are reversed, with the rat imagined to be wondering at the unnatural terror of men:

> What do you see in our eyes. . . .
> What quaver—what heart aghast?

The morning which has begun in something close to the normal pastoral mode is now enclosing images of terror—the opposite of pastoral emotions. It is the job of the end of the poem to get us back into the pastoral world, but with a difference wrought by the understanding that the sympathetic identification with the rat's viewpoint has achieved.

All the speaker's imagining has been proceeding while he was worn—preposterously, ludicrously, with a loving levity and a trace of eroticism—the poppy behind his ear. It is in roughly the place where the bullet would enter if he should stick his head up above the parapet, where the rat has scampered safely. He is aware that the poppies grow because nourished on the blood of the dead: their blood color tells him this. The poppies will finally fall just like the "athletes," whose haughtiness, strength, and fineness are of no avail. But the poppy he wears is safe for the moment—so long as he keeps his head below the parapet, hiding in a hole the way a rat is supposed to. The poppy is

> Just a little white with the dust,

the literal dust of the hot summer of 1916. It is also just a little bit purified and distinguished by having been chosen as the vehicle that has prompted the whole meditative action. But in being chosen it has been "pulled," and its death is already in train. Its apparent "safety" is as delusive as that currently enjoyed by the speaker. (Rosenberg was killed on April 1, 1918.) If it is now just a little bit white, it is already destined to be very white as its blood runs out of it. If it is now lightly whitened by the dust, it is already fated to turn wholly to "dust." The speaker is has killed it by pulling it from the parapet. The most ironic word in the poem is the *safe* of the penultimate line.

As I have tried to suggest, the poem resonates as it does because its details point to the traditions of pastoral and of general elegy. As in all elegies written out of sympathy for the deaths of others, the act of speaking makes the speaker highly conscious of his own frail mortality and the brevity of his time. Even if we do not hear as clearly as Jon Silkin the words, "Just a little while" behind "Just a little white," we perceive that the whole poem is saying "Just a little while." We will certainly want to agree with Silkin's conclusions about the poem's relation to tradition. The poem pivots on what Silkin calls "the common fantasy" about poppies, that they are red because they are fed by the blood of the soldiers buried beneath them. "It is one thing to invert," says Silkin; it is "quite another to submit one's imagination to another's, or to the collective imagination, and extend it, adding something new and harmonious."

—Paul Fussell "Arcadian Resources," *The Great War and Modern Memory* (London: Oxford University Press, 1975): pp. 251–253.

JEAN LIDDIARD ON THE PRACTICAL PROBLEMS ROSENBERG OVERCAME

[Jean Liddiard is the author of *Isaac Rosenberg: The Half Used Life* (1975) and *Working for Victory: Images of Women in the First World War, 1914–1918* (1987). In this excerpt from her biography of Isaac Rosenberg, Liddiard discusses the practical problems the war forced Rosenberg to overcome if he were to even get his poems down on paper.]

⟨. . .⟩ He could hardly pretend they were recipes for rum punch. First of all he had to find paper and something to write with—"send me a pencil or a chalk pencil" he begged his mother on 7 June 1917. The torn scraps on which his manuscripts and letters home are written bear witness to this difficulty. If he were lucky the chaplain or the canteen behind the lines would have a supply of YMCA notepaper. He then had to snatch odd moments of free time to write, as he explained to Marsh on 27 May 1917: "It is only when we get a bit of rest and the others might be gambling or squabbling I add a line or two, and continue this way." As free time occurred mainly in the evenings there was also the problem of finding light to write by. There was a chronic shortage of candles, and often Rosenberg had to wait until a fire was kindled, as he told Trevelyan earlier that winter, on 20 November 1916: "We are pretty busy and writing letters is most awkward, but after some rough days in the trenches, here before the comfortable glare of the camp fire I cannot help using these few odd minutes to answer your letter."

Once the poems were written he would send them to his sister, Annie, who would type them out and return them for him to work on. But sometimes, having managed against all the odds to finish a poem, he met the worst frustration of all, as he explained to Marsh in autumn 1916: "I have been forbidden to send poems home, as the censor won't be bothered with going through such rubbish, or I would have sent you one I wrote about our armies, which I am rather bucked about."

—Jean Liddiard, *Isaac Rosenberg: The Half Used Life* (London: Victor Gollancz, 1975): p. 209.

Works by the Poets of World War I

Wilfred Owen

Poems, ed. Siegfried Sassoon. 1920.

The Poems of Wilfred Owen, ed. Edmund Blunden, with a memoir. 1931.

Wilfred Owen: Collected Letters, ed. Harold Owen and John Bell. 1967.

Wilfred Owen: War Poems and Others, ed. Dominic Hibberd. 1973.

Wilfred Owen: The Complete Poems and Fragments, ed. Jon Stallworthy. 1983.

Wilfred Owen: Selected Letters, ed. John Bell. 1985.

The Poems of Wilfred Owen, ed. Jon Stallworthy. 1985.

Isaac Rosenberg

Night and Day. 1912.

Youth. 1915.

Moses, a Play. 1916.

Poems by Isaac Rosenberg. 1922.

The Collected Works of Isaac Rosenberg. 1949.

Works About
World War I Poets

Abercrombie, Lascelles. *The Idea of Great Poetry*. London: M. Secker 1925.

Bergonzi, Bernard. *Heroes' Twilight: A Study of the Literature of the Great War*. London: Constable, 1965.

Bewley, Marius. *Masks & Mirrors: Essays in Criticism*. New York: Atheneum, 1970.

Caesar, Adrian. *Taking It Like a Man: Suffering, Sexuality and the War Poets: Brooke, Sassoon, Owen, Graves*. New York: Manchester University Press, 1993.

Cohen, Joseph. *Journey to the Trenches: The Life of Isaac Rosenberg 1890–1918*. London: Robson Books, 1975.

———. "The Three Roles of Siegfried Sassoon." *Tulane Studies in English* 7 (1957): 169-85.

———. "The War Poet as Archetypal Spokesman." *Stand* 4, no. 3 (1960): 23–27.

———. "Owen Agonistes." *English Literature in Transition* 8, no. 5 (December, 1965): 253–68.

Corrigan, Dame Felicitas. *Siegfried Sassoon: Poet's Pilgrimage*. London: Gollancz, 1973.

Daiches, David. "The Poetry of Wilfred Owen." In *New Literary Values: Studies in Modern Literature*. Edinburgh: Oliver and Boyd, 1936.

———. *Poetry and the Modern World*. Chicago: University of Chicago Press, 1940.

———. "Isaac Rosenberg: Poet." *Commentary* 10, no. 1 (July 1950): 91–3.

Davidson, Mildred. *The Poetry Is in the Pity*. London: Chatto & Windus, 1972.

Day Lewis, Cecil. *A Hope for Poetry*. Oxford: Basil Blackwell, 1934.

Delany, Paul. *The Neo-Pagans: Friendship and Love in the Rupert Brooke Circle*. London: Macmillan, 1987.

Durrell, Lawrence. *A Key to Modern British Poetry*. Norman: University of Oklahoma Press, 1952.

Fussell, Paul. *The Great War and Modern Memory*. Oxford: Oxford University Press, 1975.

Harding, D. W. *Experience into Words*. New York: Horizon Press, 1964.

Gardner, Brian. *Up the Line to Death: The War Poets 1914–1918: An Anthology*. London: Eyre Methuen, 1964.

Giddings, Robert. *The War Poets*. New York: Orion Books, 1988.

Gose, Elliott B., Jr. "Diggin In: An Interpretation of Wilfred Owen's 'Strange Meeting.'" In *College English* 22 (March 1961).

Graham, Desmond. *The Truth of War: Owen, Blunden, Rosenberg*. Manchester: Carcanet Press, 1984

Graves, Robert. *Good-bye to All That*. New York: Doubleday Anchor Books, 1957.

Hassall, Christopher. *Rupert Brooke*. New York: Harcourt, Brace & World, 1964.

Hibberd, Dominic. *Wilfred Owen: The Last Year 1917–1918*. London: Constable and Company, 1992.

Hughes, Ted. "The Crime of Fools Exposed." *New York Times Book Review* (12 April 1964): 4, 18.

Johnston, John H. *English Poetry of the First World War: A Study in the Evolution of Lyric and Narrative Form*. Princeton, New Jersey: Princeton University Press, 1964.

Lane, Arthur. *An Adequate Response: The War Poetry of Wilfred Owen and Siegfried Sassoon*. Detroit, Mich.: Wayne State University Press, 1972.

Larkin. Philip. "The War Poet." *The Listener* (10 October 1963): 561–562.

Lehmann, John. *The Strange Destiny of Rupert Brooke*. New York: Holt, Rinehart and Winston, 1980.

Mallon, Thomas. "The Great War and Sassoon's Memory," in *Modernism Reconsidered*. ed. R. Kiely. Cambridge: Harvard University Press, 1983.

Moeyes, Paul. *Siegfried Sassoon: Scorched Glory*. London: Macmillan. 1997.

Murry, John Middleton. *The Evolution of an Intellectual*. London: Richard Cobden-Sanderson, 1920.

Parfitt, George. *English Poetry of the First World War: Contexts and Themes*. New York: Harvester Wheatsheaf, 1990.

Parsons, I. M. "The Poems of Wilfred Owen (1893–1918)." *New Criterion* 10 (July 1931): 658–669.

Pearsall, Robert Brainard. *Rupert Brooke: The Man and Poet.* Amsterdam: Editions Rodopi, 1974.

Purkis, John. *A Preface to Wilfred Owen.* New York: Addison Wesley Longman, 1999.

Quinn, Patrick J. *The Great War and the Missing Muse: The Early Writings of Robert Graves and Siegfried Sassoon.* London: Associated University Press, 1994

Roberts, Beth Ellen. "The Female God of Isaac Rosenberg: A Muse for Wartime." *English Literature in Transition 1880–1920* 39, no. 3 (1996): 319–332.

Shelton, Carole. "War Protest, Heroism and Shellshock: Siegfried Sassoon: A Case Study." *Focus on Robert Graves* 1, no. 13 (Winter 1992).

Silken, Jon. *Out of Battle: The Poetry of the Great War.* New York: St. Martin's, 1998.

———, editor. *The Penguin Book of First World War Poetry.* Second Edition. New York: Penguin Books,1996.

Stallworthy, Jon. *Wilfred Owen.* London: Oxford University Press, 1974.

Thomas, Dylan. "Wilfred Owen." In *Quite Early One Morning.* London: J. M. Dent & Sons, 1954.

Thorpe, Michael. *Siegfried Sassoon: A Critical Study.* Leiden, Netherlands: Universitaire Pers, 1966.

Van Doren, Mark. "War and Peace." *The Nation* (25 May 1921): 747.

Welland, D. S. R. *Wilfred Owen: A Critical Study.* London: Chatto & Windus, 1960.

Wilson, Jean Moorcroft. *Siegfried Sassoon: The Making of a War Poet, a Biography (1896–1918).* New York: Routledge, 1999.

Winter, Jay. *Sites of Memory, Sites of Mourning: The Great War in European Cultural History.* Cambridge, England: Cambridge University Press, 1995.

Wohl, Robert. *The Generation of 1914.* Cambridge, Mass.: Harvard University Press, 1979.

Yeats, W. B., editor. *The Oxford Book of Modern Verse.* New York: Oxford University Press, 1936.

Index of
Themes and Ideas

92; and Sassoon, 12, 13, 14, 20–21, 22, 24, 39–40, 42–44, 45, 47, 48, 49; and Shelley, 14, 24; and Sitwell, 20; universal quality of poetry of, 26–27; and war as violation of nature, 56–58; and Yeats, 9, 27, 33. See also "ANTHEM FOR DOOMED YOUTH"; "DULCE ET DECORUM EST"; "FUTILITY"; "STRANGE MEETING"

ROSENBERG, ISAAC, 63–105; and art as interpretive and unifying agent of reality, 86–88; background of as painter and images in poetry, 78–80, 97; biography of, 63–64; and Blake, 19; detached style of, 90–92; as distinguished from other war poets, 67–69; and Donne, 68, 74, 96; and exploratory habit of language, 67–68; and fascination with wounded between life and death, 93–95; and first person plural pronouns, 94; and fusion between English and Jewish culture, 76–77; and fusion of disparate attitudes, 68; "idea" in, 95–98; and Imagist demands, 96; and isolation from literary mainstream, 69–71; and Jewish tradition, 69, 70, 71, 72–73, 76–77, 82; and overcoming practical problems of war to write poems, 104–5; and Owen, 70–71, 72, 78, 81, 82, 88–90, 91, 92; and pastoral tradition conveying experience of war, 102–4; place of in English poetry, 72–73; and root image, 96, 98; and suffering, 85, 89–90; and Dylan Thomas, 72. See also "BREAK OF DAY ON THE TRENCHES"; "DEAD HEROES, THE"; "DEAD MAN'S DUMP"; "WORM FED ON THE HEART OF CORINTH, A"

"STRANGE MEETING" (OWEN), 22–35; and artistic, personal, and historical implications of war, 23; critical views on, 26–35, 43, 78; "enemy" in, 81; German in, 29, 31, 33, 34; and half-rhyme, 24–25, 61; Other in, 30–32, 33–35; and pity of war, 23, 30–33; realistic world of trenches and dream landscape in, 22; and Romanticism, 24; and spiritual death of person and society, 24; "strange" in, 22; "strange meeting" in, 22–23; stranger in, 23–24; thematic analysis of, 22–25; and truth remaining "untold," 23; "vision" in, 82

"WORM FED ON THE HEART OF CORINTH, A" (ROSENBERG), 99–105; critical views on, 101–5; and state of England developed in Rosenberg's prose work, 101–2; thematic analysis of, 99–100